Complete
English as a
Second Language
for Cambridge IGCSE®

Workbook

Chris Akhurst
Lucy Bowley

OXFORD
UNIVERSITY PRESS

OXFORD
UNIVERSITY PRESS

Great Clarendon Street, Oxford, OX2 6DP, United Kingdom

Oxford University Press is a department of the University of Oxford. It furthers the University's objective of excellence in research, scholarship, and education by publishing worldwide. Oxford is a registered trade mark of Oxford University Press in the UK and in certain other countries

© Oxford University Press 2014

British Library Cataloguing in Publication Data

Data available

978-0-19-839287-3

5 7 9 10 8 6 4

Paper used in the production of this book is a natural, recyclable product made from wood grown in sustainable forests. The manufacturing process conforms to the environmental regulations of the country of origin.

Printed in Great Britain by Bell and Bain Ltd., Glasgow

Acknowledgements

®IGCSE is the registered trademark of Cambridge International Examinations. The questions, example answers, marks awarded and/or comments that appear in this book and CD were written by the authors. In examination, the way marks would be awarded to questions like these may be different.

The publishers would like to thank the following for permissions to use their photographs:

Cover image: Happy person/Shutterstock; **p1:** bellenixe/Shutterstock; **p2:** sdecoret/Shutterstock; **p16:** iStock; **p20:** Paul Bradbury/Getty Images; **p23:** perspectivestock/Shutterstock; **p27:** meunierd/Shutterstock; **p38:** © Markus Altmann/Corbis; **p42:** © Ryan Benyi Photography/Image Source/ Corbis; **p49:** © Karen Kasmauski/Corbis; **p53:** © Michael Snell/Robert Harding World Imagery/Corbis; **p57:** © Tetra Images/Corbis; **p59:** © Bettmann/CORBIS; **p62:** © Jeffrey L. Rotman/Corbis; **p69:** © Peter Scholey/Robert Harding World Imagery/Corbis; **p71:** © Rune Hellestad/Corbis; **p73:** © Joe Toth/BPI/Corbis; **p84:** © Brad Swonetz/Corbis; **p92:** © Jonathan Blair/Corbis; **p101:** © Gianni Dagli Orti/Corbis; **p107:** © The Gallery Collection/Corbis; **p108:** © Anna Clopet/CORBIS; **p110:** © Splash News/Corbis; **p111:** REX/Forum / UIG; **p112:** Word Cloud; **p116:** iStock; **p120:** © Robin Loznak/ZUMA Press/Corbis

The author and publisher are grateful for permission to reprint extracts from the following copyright material:

Mary Bellis: 'The Life of Thomas Edison' © 2013 Mary Bellis (http://inventors. about.com/), reprinted by permission of About Inc., which can be found online at www.about.com, all rights reserved.

Floella Benjamin: excerpt from *Sea of Tears*, published by Frances Lincoln Ltd, copyright © 2011, reprinted by permission of Frances Lincoln Ltd.

Creative Choices: adapted from 'Being a puppeteer', from www.creative-choices.co.uk, reprinted by permission.

James Dorsey: adapted excerpt from '10 extraordinary burial ceremonies from around the world', reprinted by permission of the author.

Paul Eccleston: 'Denise models clothes fashioned from recycling', *The Telegraph*, © Telegraph.co.uk, reprinted by permission.

Eco Truly Park: excerpts from www.volunteeringecotrulypark.blogspot.co.uk reprinted by permission.

Esperanto: 'The Zamenhof Story' from www.esperanto.org.uk, reprinted by permission.

Frank Funaro: adapted from 'How do I play the drums?' from www. iplaythedrums.com, reprinted by permission.

Guidedogs: 'Puppy training' from www.guidedogs.co.uk, reprinted by permission.

Debbie Hadley: 'Honey Bees - roles within the Honey Bee colony' © 2013 Debbie Hadley (http://insects.about.com/), reprinted by permission of About Inc., which can be found online at www.about.com, all rights reserved.

Prof. Sarah Harkness: adapted excerpts from 'Parenting across cultures', SGI Quarterly, www.sgiquarterly.org, reprinted by permission.

Intellectual Property Office: 'What is a patent', Crown Copyright, this is public sector information licensed under the Open Government Licence v2.0.

Alison Kim: 'Roland Garros is Rafa's house', 11 June 2012, from www. ATPWorldTour.com, reprinted by permission of ATP World Tour.

Amy Kleppner: Amelia Earhart text used with permission of Amy Kleppner, as heir to the Estate of Muriel Morrissey.

Chiran Livera: 'How I became an international aid worker', 30 July 2013, www. blogs.redcross.org.uk, reprinted by permission.

Massachusetts Institute of Technology: 'Center for 21st Century Energy' from http://web.mit.edu, reprinted by permission.

Ben Miller: excerpt from *It's Not Rocket Science*, published by Sphere 2012, reprinted by permission of Little, Brown Book Group Ltd.

Simon Nkoitoi: adapted excerpt from 'The Life of a Maasai Woman', from www.ofdc.org, reprinted by permission.

Pilates Technique Certification: excerpts from www.josephpilates.com, reprinted by permission.

Laurens Rademakers: 'Why does music 'touch' us emotionally? It doesn't make sense', from www.ted.com, reprinted by permission.

David Robertson: excerpt from *Brick by Brick*, reprinted by permission of The Random House Group Limited.

Scott Polar Research Institute: excerpts from Scott's Last Expedition appear by permission of the Scott Polar Research Institute, University of Cambridge

Tom Seal: 'Sustainable supply chains: why placing ethics over profits pays off', 28 August 2013, *Guardian Professional,* copyright Guardian News & Media Ltd 2013, reprinted by permission.

Sherry Shahan: 'Life in an African Village' which appeared in *Christian Science Monitor* in 2006, reprinted by permission of the author.

The Tampa Bay Times: from 'Egypt: daily life' from http://www2.sptimes.com/ Egypt/EgyptCredit.4.2.html, reprinted by permission.

Richard Whitehead: excerpt from blog www.richardwhiteheadrunsbritain. com, reprinted by permission.

wikiHow: 'How to collect postcards' provided by wikiHow, a wiki building the world's largest, highest quality how-to manual, please edit this article and find author credits at wikiHow.com, content on wikiHow can be shared under a Creative Commons Licence.

Wikipedia: Greek marriage customs text uses material adapted from the Wikipedia article http://en.wikipedia.org/wiki/Wedding_customs_by_ country 'Wedding customs by country' which is released under the http:// creativecommons.org/licenses/by-sa/3.0/ Creative Commons Attribution-Share-Alike License 3.0.

Jennifer Wolf: 'Use Freecycle to get free household items' © 2013 Jennifer Wolf, reprinted by permission of About Inc., which can be found online at www.about.com, all rights reserved.

WWF: excerpt from Giant Panda, www.worldwildlife.org, reprinted by permission.

Zumba Fitness, LLC: information reprinted by permission.

FSC MIX Paper from responsible sources FSC® C007785

Introduction

This book has been written for students across a range of language levels and contains exercises and activities for students preparing for the Cambridge IGCSE® English as a Second Language series of examinations. The book is ideal for students who are in the earlier stages of learning English, but there is also lots of material which is aimed at refining language skills, helping students to progress towards assessment with confidence. The book contains a large amount of material which is intended to provide practice for the reading, writing, listening and speaking examinations, but also offers material which can used to practise general skills.

There are 12 chapters in this book and each one is based around a topic or theme. Chapters cover all four main language learning skills – reading, writing, listening and speaking. Exam-focused activities cement the skills students need to succeed, with extensive listening practice. In addition, the Workbook reinforces vocabulary and grammar knowledge.

 ## What's on the CD?

English as a Second Language for Cambridge IGCSE® Workbook includes a CD with additional material specifically written to support your learning:

- Audio recordings and transcripts from the Workbook

- Links to online resources: A glossary of Youtube and alternative links are provided on the CD.

Contents

1 Science and technology

 Read some fun chemistry facts and find out more about atoms, elements, gases, liquids, solids, experiments, cool chemicals, and much more.

- Hydrogen is the first element on the periodic table. It has an atomic number of 1. It is highly flammable and is the most common element found in our universe.

- Liquid nitrogen boils at 77 kelvin (−196 °C, −321 °F).

- Around 1 per cent of the sun's mass is oxygen.

- Helium is lighter than the air around us, so it floats. That's why it is perfect for the balloons you get at parties.

- Carbon comes in a number of different forms (allotropes). These include diamond, graphite, and impure forms such as coal.

- Under normal conditions, oil and water do not mix.

- Although it is still debated, it is largely recognized that the word 'chemistry' comes from an Egyptian word meaning 'earth'.

- The use of various forms of chemistry is believed to go back as far as the time of the Ancient Egyptians. By 1,000 BCE civilizations were using more complex forms of chemistry such as turning plants into medicines, extracting metal from ores, fermenting wine, and making cosmetics.

- Things invisible to the human eye can often be seen under UV light, which comes in handy for both scientists and detectives.

- Humans breathe out carbon dioxide (CO_2). Using energy from sunlight, plants convert carbon dioxide into food during a process called photosynthesis.

- Chemical reactions occur all the time, and we see them in our everyday activities such as cooking. Try adding an acid such as vinegar to a base such as baking soda and see what happens!

- Above 4 °C, water expands when heated and contracts when cooled. But between 4 °C and 0 °C it does the opposite, contracting when heated and expanding when cooled. Stronger hydrogen and oxygen bonds are formed as the water crystallizes into ice. By the time it's frozen it takes up around 9 per cent more space.

- Often formed under intense pressure over time, a crystal is made up of molecules or atoms that are repeated in a three-dimensional repeating pattern. Quartz is a well-known example of a crystal.

Check your understanding

1   Which element comes first in the periodic table?

----

2   Give two examples of different forms of carbon.

3 From which language is it generally believed the word 'chemistry' came, and what does that word mean?

----

4 How much bigger is the space taken up by frozen water than the space taken up by liquid water?

----

5 Give an example of a well-known crystal.

6* Explain which fact is your favourite.

Language focus
Comparatives and superlatives

In your student book, we looked at some comparatives. When we want to compare two objects or two people, we use the comparative form, adding '–er' to short adjectives. For example:

- Paul is shorter than Ali.

With longer adjectives, we use 'more' before the adjective to make the comparative, for example:

- That camera is more useful than the old one.

When we have more than two nouns we wish to comment on, we use the superlative form, either by adding '-est' where we would have added '-er for the comparative form; or by using 'the most' where we would have used 'more':

- I am taller than my friend and am the tallest person at the party.

- That is the most interesting book in the library.

- Ours is the most beautiful house in the street.

Insert the superlative form into these sentences, using one of the adjectives given:

friendly   calm   clean   intelligent   inspiration

1 I really like talking to people; in fact, I am the
---------------------- person in the room.

2 The restaurant is the _____ in the street.

3 Sam is very clever; actually, he is the _____ person I know.

4 It is peaceful there; in fact, it is the _____ place I know.

5 He was by far the _____ speaker I have ever heard.

It's not rocket science

What is the greatest scientific achievement there has been, in your opinion? Who has been the greatest scientist?

Building your vocabulary

distinction   privileged   self-made   galaxy   telescope   molecule   emits   spectrum

Look up the meaning of these words, read the crossword clues below, and use each one to solve the clues.

Across

3   the range

4   noteworthy

5   completed on your own

6   a small physical unit of a substance

8   a group of stars and planets

Down

1   a metal tube with glass lenses to see places far away

2   enjoying more resources than average

7   gives off

◉ Edwin Hubble

You need to know about Edwin Hubble. Not only was he arguably the most important astronomer since Galileo, but he was also an athlete. And, what is more, he has the rare **distinction** among scientists of having changed the way we think about the entire cosmos, not only once, but twice.

Everything about Hubble, from his impressive height and athletic ability to his quiet self-confidence, suggested he had a **privileged** background, but he came from a family of farmers and so was, in many ways, a **self-made** man.

He became fascinated by a particular kind of bright cloud called a nebula. It was thought at the time that the Milky Way **galaxy** was all there was to the cosmos. Hubble, working long, cold nights with a new 100-inch **telescope**, proved otherwise. He showed there were entire galaxies out there, not just our own Milky Way. He had discovered the universe.

Many people would have left it there, but Hubble was not most people. He found galaxy after galaxy, and examined the type of light they gave off. Every atom and **molecule** has a 'code' in terms of the light it **emits**. Hydrogen, which is plentiful in galaxies, gives off a characteristic ultraviolet light. Hubble noticed that these codes moved towards the red, lower end of the **spectrum**. When this happens, it generally means the object is moving away. Hubble found that the further off the galaxy, the redder its light. Running this backwards, he realized that the whole thing must have started at a single point and the universe must have had a beginning. Hubble had discovered the Big Bang.

From *It's Not Rocket Science* by Ben Miller

Check your understanding

1   Who does Ben say is perhaps the greatest scientist since Galileo?

   ----

2   Why is Hubble such a great scientist?

   ----

3   What did Hubble discover about the galaxy?

   ----

4   How are those galaxies moving?

   ----

5   What other theory does Ben say Hubble discovered?

6* Why do people want to explore the galaxies?

 Writing

Galileo, Hubble, Copernicus, and Hawking are just some of the famous scientists we have come across. But imagine that you, too, are a great scientist. What is your area of interest and what do you hope to find out about?

Write a blog about what you have discovered today and how it might just change the world.

The perfect gadget

What gadget would you put in your perfect car? What would it be able to do that no other car can do? Where in the car would you put it?

James Bond

When we think of gadgets and cars together we may think, in real life, of expensive cars like Ferraris or Aston Martins.

One of the most famous people to drive an Aston Martin is, however, fictional. James Bond, is well known for his in-car additions embodying hi-tech gadgetry, not only in Ian Fleming's novels but also in the Bond film franchise.

Anyone who has watched a Bond film will have seen one of the actors playing Bond (Sean Connery, George Lazenby, Roger Moore, Timothy Dalton, Pierce Brosnan, or Daniel Craig) either giving chase or being chased before pressing a button or flicking a switch to start a gadget and help defeat the enemy.

While the cars are remarkably robust, considering how many bumps they receive in the films, it is the gadgets in the car that are remembered as much as the make of car itself. With the push of a button, Bond's Lotus Esprit can move under water; with the flick of a switch, a parachute might come out of the back. Thanks to the inventions of Q, Bond's cars are of the very latest designs – so much so that, just sometimes, they are not even finished.

Q's gadgets come in many disguises: they are briefcases, belts, glasses, pens, and watches. We might laugh at them now, but at the time of each Bond film they were state of the art and totally believable. But although he is familiar with all these gadgets, even Bond can be fooled; he once picked up a sandwich looking for the secret gadget. But there was no secret gadget; it was just Q's lunch!

Check your understanding

1 Name one make of car that James Bond drives.

----

2 Name two of the actors who have played James Bond in a film.

----

3 What unusual thing can Bond's Lotus Esprit do?

----

4 Name two ways in which Q can disguise his gadgets.

----

5 At the time of each film, how did people view these gadgets?

6* Which gadget would you most enjoy using and why?

Patented

You have won a competition to own the patent of a recent design in technology. What are you going to choose, and why?

 Track 1.1

Listen to Ali, who works at the National Patent Office and then answer the questions that follow.

Check your understanding

1   What does a patent protect?

----

2   What might a patent holder do if someone infringes their patent?

----

3   Give one example of something the invention must have to be granted a patent.

----

4   Give an example of something which cannot be patented.

----

5   For how long does a patent last?

6* Which invention would you like to have patented and why?

◉ Thomas Edison

The first great invention developed by Edison was the tinfoil phonograph. While working to improve the efficiency of a telegraph transmitter, he noted that the tape of the machine gave off a noise resembling spoken words when played at high speed. This caused him to wonder if he could record a telephone message. He began experimenting with the telephone receiver and reasoned that the needle could prick paper tape to record a message. His experiments led him to try a stylus on a tinfoil cylinder, which, to his great surprise, played back the short message he recorded, "Mary had a little lamb."

The word phonograph was the trade name for Edison's device, which played cylinders rather than discs. The machine had two needles: one for recording and one for playback. When you spoke into the mouthpiece, the sound vibrations of your voice would be indented on to the cylinder by the recording needle. This cylinder phonograph – the first machine that could record and reproduce sound – created a sensation and brought Edison international fame.

[…]In 1878, Thomas Edison established the Edison Speaking Phonograph Company to sell the new machine. He suggested other uses for the phonograph, such as: letter writing and dictation, phonographic books for blind people, a family record (recording family members in their own voices), music boxes and toys, clocks that announce the time, and a connection with the telephone so that communications could be recorded.

However, Thomas Edison's greatest challenge was the development of a practical electric light. Contrary to popular belief, he didn't "invent" the light bulb, but rather he improved upon a 50-year-old idea. The idea of electric lighting was not new, and a number of people had worked on, and even developed, forms of electric lighting. But up to that time, nothing had been developed that was remotely practical for home use. Edison's eventual achievement was inventing not just an electric light but also an electric lighting system that contained all the elements necessary to make the light practical, safe, and economical. After one and a half years of work, success was achieved when his lamp filament burned for $13\frac{1}{2}$ hours.

There are a couple of other interesting things about the invention of the light bulb: while most of the attention was on the discovery of the right kind of filament that would work, Edison actually had to invent a total of seven system elements that were critical to the practical application of electric lights as an alternative to the gas lights that were prevalent in that day.

These were the development of:

1   the parallel circuit

2   a durable light bulb

3   an improved dynamo

4   the underground conductor network

5   the devices for maintaining constant voltage

6   safety fuses and insulating materials

7   light sockets with on-off switches.

[...]The success of his electric light brought Thomas Edison to new heights of fame and wealth, as electricity spread around the world. His various electric companies continued to grow until in 1889 they were brought together to form Edison General Electric. Despite the use of Edison in the company title, however, he never controlled this company. The tremendous amount of money needed to develop the lighting industry had needed the involvement of investment bankers.

Source: www.inventors.about.com/library/inventors/bledison.htm

Check your understanding

1   What was Edison's first great invention?

----

2   What was the message Edison first recorded on his invention?

----

3   Name two uses he suggested for his invention.

----

4   For how long did Edison work on improving the electric light bulb?

----

5   What did his electric company need to keep going?

6* What do you think was Edison's most significant achievement?

 ## Discussion point

You are in charge of the local town council, which has decided to fund a new technology college in the town.

You are going to tell the other council members:

●   why the town needs this technology college

●   where it will be in the town

●   what benefits it will bring, not only to the new students but also to the town.

Remember to use comparatives and superlatives when describing the college.

Language focus
Present simple tense

We have seen in the Student's Book the need for accuracy even with straightforward tenses; it can be easy to make a mistake when concentrating on the content we are writing about.

Practise using the present simple in these examples. Pick a verb from the list and add one to each sentence:

ask   dream   drink   cook   drive

1   I _____ every night but my friends never do.

2   My Mum _____ a great lunch when all the family gets together.

3   Dad always _____ me to call when I get home safely.

4   She _____ tea but she doesn't _____ coffee.

5   He _____ a very expensive car now he is famous.

Food and fitness

Carnivals and festivals

 1 You are advertising your local carnival for the community you live in. Write an advertising leaflet describing what will be available for people to see, do, and buy at the festival. You will need to make sure that it is appealing, so use adjectives to help give detail to the leaflet.

------------------------------- ------------------------------- -------------------------------

------------------------------- ------------------------------- -------------------------------

------------------------------- ------------------------------- -------------------------------

------------------------------- ------------------------------- -------------------------------

------------------------------- ------------------------------- -------------------------------

------------------------------- ------------------------------- -------------------------------

------------------------------- ------------------------------- -------------------------------

------------------------------- ------------------------------- -------------------------------

------------------------------- ------------------------------- -------------------------------

2 You see the advert to the carnival. What three pieces of information in the leaflet make you want to go to the carnival? List them here:

- ---

- ---

- ---

You wrote your competition entry for the Let's Cook Festival (see the student book, page 8); congratulations! You won the competition!

Now, you have been to the Let's Cook Festival. Update your blog to tell your friends about it and include the following:

- what you did at the festival
- who you went with
- which famous chef, or chefs, you met
- how you feel about your time at the festival.

Building your vocabulary

The words below appear in the restaurant review that you are about to read. Check their meanings and then use them to fill in the gaps in the practice sentences that follow.

prime   virtually   achievement   celeb   stable   renovated   influences   intrusive

When Jack was younger, he was _____ unknown; only those in his home town knew he was talented. He had several _____ on his style of acting, and even when he was famous, he never forgot those who had helped him. Then his television show moved to _____ time, and he became a well-known _____ and won many awards for his acting, although his main _____ was setting up a charity to help sick children. He also earned a lot of money, so bought a _____ which he then _____ to make into a lovely home. It was in the middle of the countryside, far away from the _____ photographers who had followed him in the city.

 Read the following restaurant review carefully, taking note of the use of the words in bold that you have practised in the previous exercise.

We went into RSJ again last night and it is still as good as ever. It has been in a **prime** location on the South Bank in London for over 30 years and in that time **virtually** every table has been booked every day it has been open. It took only a year for them to be included in *The Good Food Guide*, which is quite an **achievement**. It continues to be hugely popular with theatre-goers, as well as the occasional **celeb** – you never quite know who you will be dining with.

The restaurant itself is a former **stable** which has been lovingly **renovated** and there is plenty to do if you don't want a meal. There are regular cookery and wine courses as well.

On to the food: a mixture of European **influences** here, and all is perfectly cooked. An advantage of this restaurant is that there are always plenty of vegetables available – some restaurants serve up little more than a spoonful and charge it as a portion. Another advantage is the knowledgeable staff, who can guide but are not too pushy. The staff are attentive without being **intrusive**, and the food is expertly cooked every time. Hugely recommended!

Check your understanding

1   In which city is RSJ?

----

2   How long has the restaurant been open?

----

3   How long had it been open before it was included
    in *The Good Food Guide*?

----

4   Name one group of people who enjoy going to
    RSJ.

----

5   What was the building before it was a restaurant?

----

6   Give an example of a course you can take at RSJ.

----

7   What is the main influence on the food at RSJ?

----

8   Give one advantage of going to RSJ, according to
    the reviewer.

Now that you have read the restaurant review, underline four details in
the review that would make you want to go there.

How would you like to be a top chef for a day? Where would you
like to do this and for whom would you cook? Write a diary entry
about your perfect day as a chef. Include the name of the
restaurant you have been working in, and its location; if you have been
cooking for a private individual or family, say who they are and where
they live.

Every top chef has a signature dish – a meal for which they are famous. What would yours be? Write down your recipe in the space below, including quantities. You also need to include some adjectives, to better describe your recipe. Now blog your recipe.

Health and safety

Track 2.1

Health and safety in food are important, especially when people are paying for the food. This is why food standards officers visit every place that prepares and sells food, to check that the kitchens and eating areas are hygienically clean. Listen to a food standards officer talking about her daily life.

Check your understanding

1 Give one example of what the Food Standards Agency does.

----

2 Why do we need to use a separate thermometer to check the temperature inside a fridge?

----

3 How cold should a fridge be?

----

4 How cold should a freezer be?

----

5 Before preparing food, what do you need to do?

6* Why is it important to have a Food Standards Agency?

Speaking as a farmer

You are a farmer and a local television crew have come to your farm to ask about your farm and daily life. Here are the questions they ask you – how would you reply?

1 Why did you become a farmer?

2 What part of your job do you enjoy the most?

3 What is the hardest part of your job?

4 What one thing about your job would you change, and how?

5 What do you do in your free time?

6 What do you think the hardest part of being a farmer is?

Fitness

Track 2.2

Listen to an interview with a personal trainer at a local gym.

Check your understanding

1   What is the first thing Ash does with new gym members?

    ----

2   How often does Ben need to go for a run, according to Ash?

    ----

3   What must Ben do if he wants to use the lifting equipment?

    ----

4   How does he measure his heart rate on the running machine?

    ----

5   What is spinning?

6* What activity would you take up at the gym?

Language focus

Collocations

We need to choose the most appropriate word we can to suit our sentence context. Sometimes two words might be synonyms but, in the given context, only one fits well.

For each of the examples below, which sentence works and which does not fit? Circle the correct sentence from each pair.

1   Verbs – **make** and **do**

  • He set up the charity because he wanted to **make** a difference.

  • He set up the charity because he wanted to **do** a difference.

2   Nouns – **applause** and **clapping**

  • After the performance, there was a long round of **applause**.

  • After the performance, there was a long round of **clapping**.

3   Adjectives – **fast** and **quick**

  • He went into the restaurant but then decided to go and eat some quick food.

  • He went into the restaurant but then decided to go and eat some fast food.

Building your vocabulary

Check the meaning of the words in the following list and then substitute them for one of the synonyms (in bold) in the passage by writing them next to the word with a similar meaning.

prize-winning   martial arts   blended   recreational   self-defence   outbreak   devotee   posture

Alan was an **award-winning** _____ sportsman who was interested in **Eastern forms of**

sport _____ when it is **combined** _____ with Western forms of sport.

His interest was started after the **start** _____ of a childhood illness. The **leisure**

_____ activities he does include **learning to look after yourself** _____

and he has become a **fan** _____ of making sure he uses the correct **spine position**

_____ whenever he is at work.

 Read the following passage about the fitness guru Joseph Pilates.

Joseph Pilates was a man who believed completely in his method and practised what he said to others well into his eighties. Even as an older man, he was quite healthy until his death, at the age of 87.

In 1880 near Düsseldorf, Germany, Joseph Pilates was born to a **prize-winning** gymnast father and a mother who used natural forms of healing. As a child, Joseph suffered from several health ailments and, in an effort to restore his own health, he studied anatomy and reinforced what he learned by observing animals in the woods. Joseph studied Eastern disciplines, like yoga and **martial arts**, and **blended** them with more Western forms of physical activities, such as bodybuilding, gymnastics, boxing, and **recreational** sports – even incorporating ancient Greek and Roman forms of fitness practices.

As a young man, Joseph boxed and taught **self-defence**. In 1912 he moved to England, where he continued to box and taught self-defence at police schools. He also performed a Greek statue act in the circus with his brother, to earn money. One of the greatest examples of the immense benefits of practising Joseph Pilates' approach to health is the **outbreak** of a terrible influenza in 1918. The 1918 influenza epidemic destroyed populations all over the world. However, all those who followed Joseph's routine survived, due to their good health.

He met Clara, a nurse, and they married. Joseph and Clara taught their method of using the mind to control the muscles to a devout following in New York. Local dancers came regularly to heal injuries quickly and improve their strength while maintaining their flexibility. Choreographer George Balanchine and ballet dancer Martha Graham became **devotees** of Joseph Pilates' method.

Pilates

Breathing, proper **posture,** and the correction of various physical ailments were the focus at Joseph's studio and in his two books published in 1945. The essence of his work continues to change bodies and lives today, through his publications and those individuals committed to furthering his revolutionary ideas.

Dance companies all over the world use Pilates' exercises to keep their dancers in top form. Today his method is taught around the world in studios, gyms, in universities, and even in grade schools. Due to the attention the mainstream public gives to Hollywood celebrities, the name Pilates is now a household word, thanks to the many film and television stars who credit Pilates for their toned physique.

Source: www.Josephpilates.com

Check your understanding

1 What did Joseph Pilates' father do?

----

2 Why did Joseph study anatomy?

----

3 Name two Western forms of physical activity that influenced him.

----

4 What act did he perform at the circus?

----

5 Which ballet dancer followed Pilates' methods?

----

6 Name one of the areas that were the main focus at Pilates' studio.

----

7 When did Pilates publish his books?

----

8 Give an example of where Pilates exercises are taught today.

Sporting heroes

We read about a couple of sporting heroes in the student book, but who is your sporting hero?

Building your vocabulary

Match these words to their correct definitions. The first one has been done for you.

record   the top person in a competition

champion   what you give to something

debut   persuaded

adolescents   best achievement

contribution   young teenagers

convinced   first time at an event or competition

promotes   people who gain from something else

beneficiaries   highlights and encourages

collaborating   make happen

implement   partnering

 Read about this sporting hero and answer the questions that follow.

When Bjorn Borg won his sixth Roland Garros French Open tennis title in 1981, many believed his **record** would last forever. "Nobody ever thought that anyone would ever come close to beating that record," admitted Michael Chang, the 1989 champion. Rafael Nadal proved himself one of the clay-court greats as he lifted the Roland Garros trophy for the eighth time. "For me, it's really an honour," said the Mallorcan on court, following his victory. "Borg is one of the greatest of history, so for me, the comparison with the great Bjorn is fantastic."

Since making his Paris **debut** as an 18-year-old in 2005, Nadal has virtually owned Roland Garros. In eight appearances, he has compiled 59 wins to one loss and won the title twice without the loss of the set. Just how tough is Nadal at Roland Garros? Novak Djokovic, who nearly won all four Grand Slam titles but lost to Nadal in the final, said: "He's definitely the best player in history, on this surface, and results are showing that he's one of the best ever players of this game."

While Borg essentially retired at the age of 26, Nadal has shown no signs of slowing down. There's no telling how many more titles he could win in Paris before he hangs up his racquets. When asked whether there would be enough room to accommodate all his silverware, Nadal said with a smile, "Sure, there is space. There's always space for a Roland Garros trophy."

The Rafa Nadal Foundation was founded in November 2007. It came from the desire of the player and his family to help socially disadvantaged children and adolescents at risk of being excluded from society. Their contribution gives hope to people around the world. The headquarters for the foundation is in Manacour, Mallorca, which is also Rafa's home town.

The Rafa Nadal Foundation offers education programmes to the poor by using sport, and is convinced that sport is a basic tool of personal and social integration, which therefore becomes the main focus on which we base our actions. It also promotes personal training for each of its beneficiaries: the spirit of achievement, effort, respect, and trust.

The foundation is currently collaborating with foundations and organizations that have proven experience in similar projects. They join together to implement new integration and development programmes, both nationally and internationally.

Source: www.atpworldtour.com

Check your understanding

1 Before Nadal, who was one of the greatest clay-court tennis players?

----

2 When did Nadal first play the French Open tennis championship?

----

3 How many matches has he lost at the French Open, according to the article?

----

4 When did he start the Rafa Nadal Foundation?

----

5 Why did he start the Rafa Nadal Foundation?

----

6 In which town is the Rafa Nadal Foundation based, and why?

----

7 What does the foundation use to help young people?

----

8 Give an example of who the foundation collaborates with.

Angus Macfadyen

Track 2.3

Other sporting heroes are less internationally known than Nadal. In the student book, we read about Angus, who ran the London Marathon on crutches. But what did he do next?

As a non-swimmer, there was an obvious choice for Angus – his next feat for charity would be to swim across the English Channel, a 21-mile swim between England and France. Listen to the interview with Angus.

Check your understanding

1 What made Angus decide to swim the Channel?

----

2 How far could Angus swim after six months?

----

3 How long is the Channel swim?

----

4 Apart from swimming, name two things Angus did to help his training.

----

5 Give three words Angus uses to describe the Channel swim.

6* Think of three adjectives which could be used to describe Angus' achievement.

Fitness trends

Building your vocabulary

Choose and circle one word from the three given which gives a close synonym to the words in the left-hand column, which you will also see in the reading text below. The first one has been done for you.

global — large / (worldwide) / popular

exhilarating — exciting / interesting / unusual

blend — add / include / mix

quarterly — four times per year / twice a year / once a year

impact — change / influence / design

initiatives — thoughts / plans / ideas

motor neurone disease — disease mainly affecting the muscles / disease mainly affecting the heart / disease mainly affecting the bones

vision — idea for the future / past plans / present hopes

 Read the following passage about Zumba, a recent fitness trend.

Founded in 2001, Zumba Fitness is a **global** lifestyle brand that mixes fitness, entertainment and culture into an **exhilarating** dance-fitness sensation! Zumba® exercise classes are "fitness-parties" that **blend** upbeat world rhythms with easy-to-follow choreography, for a total-body workout that feels like a celebration. We offer different types of Zumba classes, plus DVD workouts, original music collections, clothing and footwear, video games, interactive Fitness-Concert™ events, **a quarterly** lifestyle magazine, and more.

Are you ready to party? Forget the workout, just lose yourself in the music and find yourself in shape at the original dance-fitness party. Zumba® classes feature exotic rhythms set to high-energy Latin and international beats. Before you know it, you'll be getting fit and your energy levels will be soaring! It's easy to do, effective and totally exhilarating.

14 million people now do Zumba worldwide, in 151 countries and in 140,000 locations.

Each day around the world, the Zumba® program makes a positive **impact** on millions of people's lives, and it's in this spirit that Zumba Love was founded. The mission of Zumba Love is to foster charitable **initiatives** that raise funds and awareness for important global health causes, and to celebrate the joy of giving through dance, fitness, friendship, and love.

Powered by the energy and passion of our Zumba Instructor Network (ZIN™) and Zumba fans worldwide, Zumba Love has raised millions of dollars for breast cancer, **motor neurone disease**, heart health and more through thousands of Zumbathon® charity events and other Zumba activities. And this is only the beginning. Zumba Love will touch more and more people around the world as we continue to grow our **vision**.

Source: www.zumba.com

Check your understanding

1 In which year did Zumba start?

----

2 Give two examples of things which combine to make Zumba.

----

3 How often is the Zumba magazine published?

----

4 In how many countries is Zumba available?

----

5 Name one cause Zumba Love has helped.

6* Why do people enjoy Zumba?

Discussion topic

Your class is opening a gym in your local area. Divided into four groups, you will contribute to the success of the opening in different ways:

- **Group One** will plan which fitness classes will be available at the gym. Make a list, including how long each class will be, how much each class costs, and an explanation of how people can book to go.

- **Group Two** will plan which music will be suitable for each class and how it will be played during the class. Each class will be different, so make sure you choose appropriate music for each class. You also need to decide what music will be playing in the changing rooms and other public areas of the gym.

- **Group Three** will decide what other facilities will be available at the gym (for example, a café) and how much of a discount members will get when they go there.

- **Group Four** will design ways of promoting the gym before it opens, with leaflets and posters. Include a discount voucher and an explanation of how to use it and by when.

Language focus
Past simple tense

We have seen some examples of how to use the past simple in the Student's Book. Now, here is some more practice.

First, change the verb into the correct form of the regular past simple:

1 We (cook) a wonderful meal for our parents last night.

2 I (like) strawberries when I was younger

3 He never (brush) his teeth when he was a small boy and now they are falling out.

4 They (touch) the stone and were surprised to feel it was warm.

5 Every spring, my mother (clean) the house from top to bottom.

Now, change the verb into the correct form of the irregular past simple:

1 I (go) to town and (see) my Mum.

2 I (drink) coffee when I was younger but I don't any more.

3 She (take) some fantastic photos of the mountains.

4 He (be) a chef and so (cook) some very tasty meals.

5 They (have) a dog and then they (buy) a cat.

Communities

Insect colonies

The sight of a colony of ants working together to cut up and carry off items of food is impressive. So is the way in which they rush to defend their territory and to repair damage done to it. But they are not the only insects from whom we can learn about communities. The honey bee community is impressive, too, especially in ways that contribute to the manufacture of honey.

Building your vocabulary

Check the meaning of these words and then match the words to the definitions on the right. These are the meanings employed in the passage that you are going to read. The first one has been done for you.

caste system	a massed colony
assume	unpleasant task
drone	fight between two
sterile	of the body
duel	different classes in society
anatomical	wax structure containing honey
chore	convert to liquid
comb	to take on
evaporate	infertile
swarm	male bee

 Honey bees

Roles within the honey bee colony

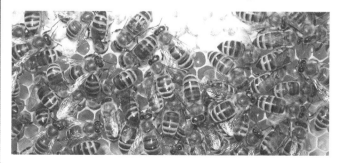

Honey bees employ a caste system to accomplish the tasks that ensure the survival of the colony. Each member of the community fulfills a need that serves the group. Tens of thousands of worker bees, all females, assume responsibility for feeding, cleaning, nursing, and defending the group. Male drones live only to mate with the queen, who is the only fertile female in the colony. The queen need not lift a wing, as workers tend to her every need.

The Queen

Don't get the idea that the queen is lazy, though. A newly hatched queen begins her life in a duel to the death with any other queens present in the colony, and must destroy potential rivals that have not yet hatched. Once she accomplishes this, she takes her virgin mating flight. Throughout her life, she lays eggs and secretes a chemical that keeps all the other females in the colony sterile.

Drones

The drone's anatomical structure proves its limited role in the colony. Drones lack stingers, so they cannot help defend the hive. Without structures for collecting pollen or nectar, they cannot contribute to feeding the community. After mating with the queen, its only reason for existence, the drone dies. In the autumn, worker bees prevent the drones from entering the hive, effectively starving them to death.

Workers

Female worker bees accomplish every chore unrelated to reproduction. In their first days, workers tend to the queen. For the remainder of their short lives, workers keep busy – hence the expression 'busy bees'. They build the comb in which honey is stored and eggs are laid. Workers collect pollen and nectar, and evaporate the nectar to make honey for times when food is scarce. They tend to the queen, the young drones, and the larvae. When threatened, the workers defend the colony. New research suggests that the workers also make the collective decision to move the colony, or swarm.

Source: www.insects.about.com/od/antsbeeswasps/p/ honeybeesociety.htm

Check your understanding

1   Who looks after the queen?

    ----

2   What is the first thing a new queen does?

    ----

3   How does she prevent other queens from hatching?

    ----

4   What two things are stored in the comb?

    ----

5   Which bees defend the hive against attack?

6* What examples of teamwork among bees most impress you?

 ## A visit to the bees

Imagine that a friend of yours is a beekeeper. You are invited to watch him as he looks after them. Suitably clad in protective clothing so the bees won't sting you, you follow him as he shows you inside one of his hives. As he does so, he explains how a colony of bees works. After your visit, you post a blog describing your day and expressing your admiration for the bees. Write that blog.

Language focus

Active and passive verbs

In the student book we looked at the two different voices used for verbs:

Active: "The worker bees defend the colony."

Passive: "The colony is defended by the worker bees."

See if you can identify which voice the following sentences are written in. For each one, say whether the verbs used are active or passive.

		Active	Passive
1	My father kept bees in the small vegetable patch behind our house.	☐	☐
2	All the honey we ate was produced by his bees.	☐	☐
3	Everyone who visited us was given a jar of honey that he had extracted from his honeycombs.	☐	☐
4	He was sometimes stung by one of his bees but he never complained about them.	☐	☐
5	"That's one less worker to look after the queen," he used to say.	☐	☐

Can you change these sentences so that the active voice is passive, and vice versa?

Human communities

⊙ Life in a Maasai Kraal

Village life in the Maasai region of Kenya gives us a picture of a community that has continued unchanged for centuries.

Building your vocabulary

Check the meaning of these words and then see if you can fit them into the sentences that follow.

kraal   igloo   ochre   whisk   draped

1 A Maasai village is called a _____.

2 The _____ stained his hands bright red.

3 He had an interesting fly _____ made from the tail of a giraffe.

4 The dome of an _____ was just visible in the snow.

5 He wore his tribal cloak _____ casually over his shoulders.

◀ ▶ ↻ ✕ 🏠 🌐 _____ 🔍

Nkadaru and family

Several families have huts in this Maasai **kraal**. Nkadaru and his sister helped their mother build their **igloo**-shaped hut by weaving long tree branches into sturdy walls. Nkadaru plugged the gaps with grass and leaves to keep out sun and rain. His mother mixed cattle dung and mud in a bucket. Together the family plastered the walls with the clay.

Nkadaru's sister helps their mother with her many activities – patching the hut, making clothes, milking animals, stringing beads, and tending to their small plot of beans and corn. She ties ribbons on their baby brother to show how special he is.

When Nkadaru is older, he – like his brother – won't herd baby animals. Young warriors have more important duties, such as protecting the village from lions and water buffalo.

Like all warriors in this village, his brother wears his long hair in braids. He decorates himself with beaded jewellery made by women friends. A thin bone pierces one ear and a button made from a crocodile-egg shell shines in his hair. He paints his skin with **ochre**, a reddish clay ground up and mixed with animal fat.

Nkadaru's mother stitches hides into clothing, shoes, and bedcoverings. She also makes jewellery for the family. Her head is shaved to draw attention to a collar of beads on her neck. She earns extra money by selling beadwork to foreigners.

The beads reflect colours in nature. Blue is like the sky and green is a symbol of peace, a reminder of the healthy plants after it rains.

Her beaded earrings are similar to a wedding ring, because only married women wear them.

Nkadaru is happy when people from other countries visit his kraal. Sometimes they bring gifts: pens, ribbons, balloons, or balls.

Nkadaru's father is an elder, belonging to a council that governs the village. Their duties involve making important decisions and solving problems.

Elders wear beaded jewellery and decorate their bodies for special ceremonies. They carry simple items, including a walking cane and a buffalo-tail fly **whisk** used for blessings. A thick cotton blanket is **draped** over their strong shoulders.

Nkadaru's day passes quickly. Near dusk, he herds baby goats through the open gate into the village. The goats curl up inside the hut. His mother boils water for tea over a small fire. His sister brings in cow's milk and fresh corn.

Nkadaru and his brother settle in beside their father and listen to stories about the Maasai people. Nearby mountains cast shadows over the village, as if trying to protect their ancient way of life.

Source: www.csmonitor.com/2006/1107/ p18s02-hfes.html

Check your understanding

1 Who built Nkadaru's family's hut?

----

2 What are the huts made of?

----

3 What crops do the family grow?

----

4 What does Nkadaru's older brother help to protect the village from? Two examples are given.

----

5 What does Nkaradu's father wear to show that he is an elder?

6* In what ways is colour important to the Maasai community?

✏ Note-taking – part 1

The account of Nkaradu's village life gives us an interesting picture of a community at work. Read through the passage again and, as you do so, note down all the things mentioned that contribute to that community under the following headings:

All his family play their part	How the village is organized	What they live on
------------------------------	------------------------------	------------------------------
------------------------------	------------------------------	------------------------------
------------------------------	------------------------------	------------------------------
------------------------------	------------------------------	------------------------------

A day in a Maasai mother's life

Track 3.1

Listen to the account that a Maasai gives of a typical day in his mother's life. Then answer the multiple-choice questions that follow, choosing the most appropriate answer in each case. Write the letter of the correct answer in the box provided.

1   Why is the rain welcome?

   A   It shows where the leaks in the roof are.

   B   It brings to an end several months' drought.

   C   It enables the mother to make mud.

2   On average, how many cows does each woman milk?

   A   10

   B   15

   C   between 10 and 15

3   What is their main food?

   A   Milk

   B   Vegetables

   C   Beef

4   What dangers are encountered when collecting firewood?

   A   Fire

   B   Dangerous animals

   C   Floods

5   Who collects the water?

   A   Mother

   B   Children

   C   Men

 Note-taking – part 2

Listen to the account again. You can now add to the notes you made earlier with additional points about the Maasai community.

Who has the main responsibility in the community? Who makes decisions?	Who does most of the work?	How are the children involved?
-----------------------------	-----------------------------	-----------------------------
-----------------------------	-----------------------------	-----------------------------
-----------------------------	-----------------------------	-----------------------------
-----------------------------	-----------------------------	-----------------------------

A Maasai village community

Using the notes you have made, write a paragraph about that village community.

Building a community

Remote village communities can seem very attractive and it is tempting to want to join them – or to start communities of our own. If you were starting a new community, where might you choose to place it? What would it be like?

The people writing the next article have done just that.

Building your vocabulary

Check the meaning of these words and then see if you can complete the crossword that follows.

strategically   elevated   tolerance   located   consciousness   marginalized   interns

operational   agronomist   humus

Across

1   nutritious soil

3   respect for others' opinions

6   raised; higher

8   students; trainees

9   found

10 agricultural expert

Down

2   chosen for a particular purpose

4   moved to the edges

5   open for business

7   awareness

Read about a group of people who have set up their own community.

Welcome to the Eco Truly Park – Peru

Eco Truly Park is a beautiful Peruvian Pacific coast ecological, artistic community strategically located on Chacra y Mar beach, a district of Aucallama, in the province of Huaral, one hour by bus or car (63 km) north of the capital city, Lima. We live together according to principles of non-violence, simple living, and elevated thinking, and visitors can learn and experience how it is possible to live happily in harmony with nature, others, and themselves. We are looking for people who are basically open-minded and want to practise tolerance, compassion, and patience.

The architecture and values of the community are in part inspired by Indian traditional teachings and lifestyle. We are the first ecological educational centre of Peru. We have inspired similar successful projects in neighbouring countries such as Chile, Ecuador, Colombia, and Bolivia. The community is located at 2.5 m above sea level and consisted previously of completely sandy, unworkable land. In the last 18 years we have developed a unique organic-awareness cultivation and ecological programme run by an increasing number of residents and volunteers, with the goal of becoming fully sustainable and self-sufficient.

Become a happy person, enjoy helping without stress.

Today our community is visited by the people from Lima and all over the world, who are able to experience an alternative way of life. The surrounding area of Huaral has thus been positively influenced in terms of the development of ecological consciousness. According to recent professional studies, Eco Truly Park programmes have become a model of sustainable alternative solutions for the extreme poverty of more than half of the Peruvian citizens (over 14 million people) living in rural and urban marginalized villages. Nowadays, Eco Truly Park is also recognized as an important tourist destination by local government and the Peruvian media.

Volunteers are allowed to stay at Eco Truly for as long as they wish. To get the most out of their experience, we estimate interns will want to commit themselves to at least four hours a day. Volunteers of all ages and backgrounds are welcome to join us; the only requirement is that you are enthusiastic about working with our community. Our basic accommodation is separate shared rooms for men and women; if you would prefer a separate, individual room in our hostel, we can provide that service for a slight cost.

We have a number of workshops that you can take advantage of, including yoga, art, and Vedic philosophy. You are also more than welcome to help out in our kitchen, vegetarian restaurant or bakery (operational two days a week). If you are willing to get dirty, you can work on our organic farm with our agronomist, who also teaches theoretical and practical classes on organic agriculture, preparation of humus, and composting. More than anything we hope that you make new friends, and have the experience of a lifetime.

People come here from all over the world, so we try and help out as much as possible to accommodate language difficulties.

Source: www.volunteeringecotrulypark.blogspot.co.uk

Check your understanding

1 How far is it to the capital city from Eco Truly Park?

----

2 What other South American countries have similar projects to the Eco Truly Park? Name two others:

----

3 What was the area like before the park was founded there?

----

4 Explain briefly how the project has helped relieve poverty in Peru.

----

5 What adjectives might you use to summarize the experience of staying at the Eco Truly Park?

✎ Shall we go?

Read again the passage advertising Eco Truly Park. Does it appeal to you? Imagine that the Eco Truly organization opens a similar park somewhere not far from you. Send an email to a friend, *either* urging him/her to consider going with you *or* explaining why you will not be going.

💬 Discussion topic

So what *does* make a community? Is it the setting? Or the people? Does it need careful organization? Or does it just happen?

Go back to the list of ingredients that you suggested at the start of Chapter 3 of your student book. Have you changed your mind? What might you add to your earlier list? Why?

Discuss and agree on your top ten tips for a successful community.

Animals and us

Keeping pets

Keeping any pet is rewarding but it is also a responsibility. Animals have needs that must be considered, as must questions of welfare and safety. What advice would you give to pet owners?

Building your vocabulary

Check the meaning of these words and match those in the left-hand column to those in the right-hand column.

bonds	made
forged	left behind
nurtured	what you do
behavioural	regular
preventive	nourished
abandoned	avoiding
suitability	living conditions
consistent	things to consider
environment	appropriateness
factors	close friendships

Now use each one in a sentence to show the meaning.

Read the following article on advice for owning pets.

Advice for responsible pet owners

Taking any pet into a home to become part of a family can be hugely rewarding. Special bonds are forged as respect and friendship are learned and nurtured. However, allowing any pet to share your home is a huge undertaking that requires careful consideration. All pets require time, money, and commitment, so it's important to be honest with yourselves about how much you have of each.

All pets have basic needs. The five animal welfare needs are:

Behaviour
Your pet should be allowed to express the normal behavioural patterns of its species and breed.

Companionship
Your pet should be housed on its own or with other animals in a way that suits its species or breed.

Diet
Your pet has a need to be fed a healthy and consistent diet, including clean, fresh water.

Environment
Your pet should be provided with a suitable place to live that offers a safe environment, with room to move.

Health
Your pet has a right to have any illness or injury properly treated.

It is the responsibility of all pet owners to understand the needs of their pet and to ensure that they remain healthy and loved throughout their lives. Behavioural problems should be understood and preventive measures put in place. Only when all pet owners take responsibility will all pets be raised to become pleasant, well-behaved companions for owners and society members.

Choice of pet
It is advisable for prospective pet owners to carefully consider all factors before they select a pet that would best suit their lifestyles and perceived needs. Wrong choices can lead to pets showing inappropriate behaviour, which often results in them being abandoned, sent to animal shelters, or returned to breeders or the original owners.

Source: www.peteducationtrust.com/responsible-pet-ownership-advice

Check your understanding

1   According to the advice, what two things are learned by having a pet?

   ----

2   What three requirements should you consider when thinking of having a pet?

   ----

3   What other animals can be housed alongside your pet?

   ----

4   What are a pet's dietary requirements?

   ----

5   What, according to the advice, can lead to pets being abandoned?

6*   Explain briefly what advice given here might persuade someone that a pet is not for them.

Advice to a pet owner

You have been asked to compile brief guidelines for pet owners in your community. These are meant to be very general, covering such areas as health, safety, consideration of neighbours, and welfare of the animal. Complete this card:

Advice to a pet owner

1 ---

2 ---

3 ---

4 ---

5 ---

Language focus

Many animals are seen as symbols of the characteristics they are thought to have. So, for example, a lion is seen to symbolize bravery and a donkey (or a mule) stubbornness. This is seen in the following expressions:

1 Hector was as brave as a lion.

2 "You are a stubborn donkey," she said.

What characteristics do you think the following might be seen as symbols of?

elephant   ox   cow   bee   eel

rhinoceros   crocodile

Compose sentences using the animal as a symbol of the characteristic you thought it might have. In doing so, you will be writing either **similes** (like sentence 1) or **metaphors** (like sentence 2), as is explained in the student book on page 82. Put an S or an M after each sentence you write, to say which you think it is.

 Talented animals that help disabled people are useful because they have been carefully trained. What sort of training do you think they might need to help blind or partially sighted people?

Building your vocabulary

Check the meaning of these words and then see if you can fill in the spaces in the sentences that follow.

sponsor   negotiate   obstacles   gradually   navigate   treat   misconception

napping   immunization   crucial   harness   kerb

Marc's friends were keen to _____ him once they realised how _____ a good guide dog was to help him get about. They paid for the puppy's _____, presented Marc with a _____ for the puppy and _____ him to a place on the training programme. No one was under the _____ that it would be quick or easy but _____ Marc and Grip learned to _____ the walk to the shops. The only _____ to be _____ was one road that had to be crossed. Grip would approach the _____, wait patiently and check carefully that all was clear before venturing to cross. They became an inseparable team as Marc relied on Grip more and more and Grip was never caught _____ when his master called.

◎ Puppy training

How do you make a guide dog?

It doesn't happen overnight. And it takes patience, time… and money. Did you know, for instance, that each guide-dog partnership involves 20 months of training, seven years of support – and costs around £50,000? You'll find out more about how it all works if you sponsor your own guide dog puppy, but for now, here are two interesting features of guide-dog puppy training.

Negotiating obstacles

We introduce the dogs to obstacles gradually, and teach them to navigate their way round. It can take a while to master, but when the dogs get it right the trainer gives them lots of encouragement and maybe even a little treat!

They can't check the traffic lights!

It's a popular misconception that a guide dog will know when to cross the road by waiting for the green light. In reality, it's a team effort – and not an easy task. On a standard kerb-to-kerb crossing known to the owner, the guide dog is trained to stop at the edge, to indicate it has reached a crossing. The owner will listen for traffic, then, when he or she decides it's safe, give the command "Forward!" However, the guide dog's training teaches them NOT to obey the command if a car's coming.

0 to 6 weeks

Your tiny puppy is living with its mum and siblings in a guide dog volunteer's home. As well as playing, exploring and napping, the puppy will go to our state- of-the-art breeding centre at six weeks for health checks and immunizations.

6 weeks to 4 months

Your puppy has now moved to its puppy walker's home. During these crucial months, the dog will start learning good manners and basic commands, such as "sit" and "down" – as well as how to walk on the lead.

4 to 14 months

Your puppy is starting to get used to the area it lives in. It will learn how to negotiate flights of stairs, busy shopping areas and various means of transport. It will also get used to being around people and other dogs.

14 to 17 months

It's time for guide-dog training school. A professional guide-dog trainer will introduce your puppy to a special brown training harness. It's also time to start learning guiding skills such as dealing with kerbs and avoiding obstacles.

17 to 20 months

At this stage, a guide-dog mobility instructor will start to pull all your puppy's training together, so that it learns to use guiding skills in everyday situations. They will also start the matching process, finding a blind or partially sighted person who's just right for your puppy.

20 to 22 months

Congratulations – you are the sponsor of a fully trained guide dog! He or she will now be matched with a person with sight loss so they can get to know each other and start their partnership training.

22 to 24 months

Your guide dog has changed a blind or partially sighted person's life forever! It has now settled into its new home and is practising its regular routes. A guide-dog mobility instructor will keep visiting to check how it's all going.

Source: www.guidedogs.org.uk/sponsorapuppy/puppy-training/#.Ugn5GZJJOVU

Check your understanding

1 What three things are involved in training guide dogs?

----

2 How long does it take to train the dogs?

----

3 What do people mistakenly think guide dogs can do?

----

4 When is a guide dog trained to disobey its owner's command?

----

5 At what age are puppies introduced to their future owners?

6* "Your guide dog has changed a blind person's life forever!" Briefly in your own words describe the difference having a guide dog will make to a blind person's life.

Listening in

Track 4.1

Listen to an interview in which a guide dog owner talks about her dog, then answer the multiple-choice questions below. Circle the correct answer from A, B, or C in each case.

1 Which best describes Maxine? Is she:

   A blind in one eye

   B completely sightless

   C partially sighted

2 How many guide dogs has she had?

   A one

   B two

   C three

3 What was wrong with her first dog?

   A too slow to respond

   B too quick to respond

   C bad tempered

4 What is Trixy's main job?

   A to stop Maxine walking into things

   B to take her shopping

   C to be a good guard dog

5 What has Trixy given back to Maxine?

   A her eyesight

   B a lifeline

   C her confidence

Descriptions

Maxine's life has been dramatically improved by the arrival of Trixy. She is certainly a remarkable dog, providing a valuable service. How would you describe her? Write three short paragraphs describing Trixy, each one from a different point of view. Use the prompts provided for each paragraph.

Imagine that you are the guide-dog for the blind instructor:

Imagine that you are Maxine's neighbour:

Imagine that you are Maxine herself:

The World Wildlife Fund

 Do you think it is important to protect species that are in danger of disappearing and becoming extinct? Why? Does it apply to all endangered animals, or just some?

Building your vocabulary

Check the meaning of these words and then see if you can complete the crossword.

subsist   function   bulk   logging   encroachment   monitoring   furry

integral   founding

Across

3 large size

4 cutting down trees

6 beginning

7 checking

8 do the job of

Down

1 moving into another's space

2 live off

5 an essential part of

8 covered in fur

Perhaps the most famous endangered species to be protected by the World Wildlife Fund (the WWF) is the one which gives the fund its logo, the giant panda.

◉ The giant panda

This peaceful creature with a distinctive black-and-white coat is adored by the world and considered a national treasure in China. The bear also has a special significance for WWF. The panda has been WWF's logo since our founding in 1961.

The rarest member of the bear family, pandas live mainly in bamboo forests high in the mountains of western China, where they subsist almost entirely on bamboo. They must eat from 26 to 84 pounds of it every day, a formidable task for which they use their enlarged wrist bones that function as thumbs.

Newborn pandas are about 1/900th the size of their mother – but can grow to up to 330 pounds as adults. These bears are excellent tree-climbers despite their bulk.

WWF was the first international conservation organization to work in China at the Chinese government's invitation. WWF's main role in China is to assist and influence policy-level conservation decisions through information collection, demonstration of conservation approaches, communications, and capacity building.

Protecting giant pandas

We work towards and advocate for:

- increasing the area of panda habitat under legal protection

- creating green corridors to link isolated pandas

- patrolling against poaching, illegal logging, and encroachment

- building local capacities for nature reserve management

- continued research and monitoring.

WWF has been helping with the Chinese government's National Conservation Programme for the giant panda and its habitat. Thanks to this programme, panda reserves now cover more than 3.8 million acres of forest.

The WWF logo

The inspiration for the WWF logo came from Chi-Chi, a giant panda that arrived at the London Zoo in 1961, the same year that WWF was created. WWF's founders were aware of the need for a strong, recognizable symbol that would overcome all language barriers. They agreed that the big, furry animal with her appealing, black-patched eyes would make an excellent logo.

The design of the logo has evolved over the past four decades, but the giant panda's distinctive features remain an integral part of WWF's treasured and unmistakable symbol. Today, WWF's trademark is recognized as a universal symbol for the conservation movement.

Source: www.worldwildlife.org/species/giant-panda

Language focus

Future tense

Practise the accurate use of the Future Tense by changing the following passage from the present to the future, so that it refers to 'tomorrow' rather than "today".

Today is my birthday and I am celebrating it at the zoo. I watch the pandas playing. It is their first day on view to the public. My sister is here, too. She is staying with me for the week and is keen to see the pandas. She loves their cuddly appearance and wants to take one home with her! My brother can't be with us as he is working in London this week and cannot get time off to join us. I miss him but am enjoying the day with my sister.

Now write a short paragraph beginning 'In ten years' time I shall be …' making as much use of the Future Tense as you can. Please use a separate sheet of paper. Then compare your paragraph with your neighbour.

Check your understanding

1 In what year was the World Wildlife Fund started?

----

2 What is the panda's main food?

----

3 How does WWF guard against pandas becoming cut off from other pandas?

----

4 What has been achieved as a result of the Chinese National Conservation Programme?

----

5 What does the WWF panda logo stand for?

6* The panda is "adored by the world". Why is this, according to the whole passage?

What is the World Wildlife Fund?

You have been asked by a friend what the WWF does. As you have just read about the pandas, you send your friend an email explaining briefly what you have found out about the WWF from the article. What will you say?

Aesop's fables

Aesop's fables use animals to tell stories. They are usually short and simple and are intended to give us something to think about. Two of his best-known stories are used in spoken English work in the student book. Here is another well-known fable.

Belling the cat

Long ago, the mice had a general council to consider what measures they could take to outwit their common enemy, the Cat. Some said this, and some said that; but at last a young mouse got up and said he had a proposal to make, which he thought would meet the case.

"You will all agree," said he, "that our chief danger consists in the sly and treacherous manner in which the enemy approaches us. Now, if we could receive some signal of her approach, we could easily escape from her. I venture, therefore, to propose that a small bell be procured, and attached by a ribbon round the neck of the Cat. By this means we should always know when she was about, and could easily retire while she was in the neighbourhood."

This proposal met with general applause, until an old mouse got up and said: "That is all very well, but who is to bell the Cat?" The mice looked at one another and nobody spoke. Then the old mouse said:

"It is easy to propose impossible remedies."

Source: www.aesopfables.com/cgi/aesop1.cgi?
1&BellingtheCat&&bellcat2.ram

Reading aloud

This is an excellent short story to read out loud. Spend time practising your reading of it and find someone to read it to. Think about the ways in which you can bring out the point of the story by how you read. Better still, memorize it so that you can tell it in your own words.

Now it's your turn

Try writing a short story with a moral.

You could choose to update the story "Belling the Cat" by putting it in a modern setting, or you may prefer to write your own fable using animals for characters.

Discussion topic

Your class has decided to sponsor an endangered animal, but this raises a number of questions:

- Which animal should you choose? It could be a tiger, a giant panda, or something more unusual, a local species that is under threat, perhaps.

- How are you going to raise awareness of this animal and its needs?

- What money-raising activities might you organize?

This also raises the important question:

- Why sponsor an animal at all? Are there not more deserving things to spend money on?

Discuss your answers to these questions as a group.

Working life

Summary jobs

Have you ever had a summer job – the chance to earn some pocket money or to do something different over the holiday period? What did you do? Or perhaps you haven't yet had the opportunity. If you could choose, what would you try your hand at?

Building your vocabulary

Check the meaning of the following words and then fill in the blanks in the paragraph that follows.

prime   typically   eligible   interact   elementary   shift   caddie   survey   anonymous   retail

John spent his summer as a _ _ _ _ _ _ _ on the local golf course. He worked the morning _ _ _ _ _ _ from 0800 to 1200, which left him free to _ _ _ _ _ _ _ _ _ with the friends he made there. His _ _ _ _ _ _ reason was to make money and he _ _ _ _ _ _ _ _ _ earned £50 a morning and even received a large tip from an _ _ _ _ _ _ _ _ _ _ _ visitor in return for completing a _ _ _ _ _ _ _ about his choice of golf balls. He was _ _ _ _ _ _ _ _ to play in the _ _ _ _ _ _ _ _ _ _ _ competition in which his opponents were _ _ _ _ _ _ _ workers on their day off from their shops.

Read the following text and answer the questions that follow.

Summer jobs for 16-year-olds

Summer is prime time for teenagers to make money: with no schoolwork, students are often available to work full-time during these months. There are quite a few summer jobs for 16-year-olds that you might be interested in, be they for yourself or for your teenage son/daughter.

Working in retail

Typically, 16-year-olds can begin working in retail stores, although the laws can vary. The positions include cashier or shop assistant. This is a job worth considering if you like dealing with people. Check with your local authority to determine age restrictions and whether a worker's permit is necessary.

Lifeguard

If you like to swim, junior lifeguard is another position for which a 16-year-old may be eligible. You'll get to spend time outdoors at the beach or the pool. This job requires knowing basic first aid and how to handle various emergencies, and the ability to stay calm in a crisis.

Babysitter

Babysitting is very popular among summer jobs for 16-year-olds to explore when school is out. Babysitters must monitor children closely to ensure their safety. Many children are eager to interact with their babysitters, and so babysitters should be friendly and open to elementary-level games. The job may be fairly demanding, as children need constant attention. Hence, it is recommended for highly responsible teens that are fond of kids.

Restaurant worker

Depending on the laws in your area, you may be able to be legally hired by a restaurant. Many teens start their working years in restaurants, often at fast-food establishments. At a restaurant such as McDonald's, you can work as a cashier or food preparer. At fancier restaurants, you may work as a shift person who cleans tables or as a dishwasher. Sometimes a 16-year-old can become a waiter or waitress, but often you need to be a few years older to get these jobs.

Other choices

Summer jobs for 16-year-olds can also take the form of newspaper rounds, car washes, assistants in buildings and offices, and caddies at golf courses. Large workplaces like hospitals also offer ample employment opportunities because they employ many workers.

You can also choose online jobs like survey-filling. You will be paid for carrying out short, anonymous surveys on things like movies, magazines, TV, and hundreds of other products and topics.

Above are some suggestions of summer jobs for 16-year-olds. We hope you find them useful, and we wish you luck in finding a job this coming summer!

Source: Adapted from www.thejobsfor16yearolds.com/ summer-jobs-for-16-year-olds

Check your understanding

1 Why are teenagers available at this time?

----

2 Who is particularly suited to retail work?

----

3 Apart from swimming ability, what else is required to be a lifeguard?

----

4 What must a babysitter do to ensure children's safety?

----

5 What job is it suggested you can do online?

6* Which of these summer jobs would you choose, and why?

 # Diary entry

Imagine that you are 16 (perhaps you are!) and take on one of these summer jobs. Write your diary entries for the first and last days of your employment.

As you began, did you:

- feel nervous or excited, or both?
- find it easy or daunting?
- feel glad to have signed up, or wish you hadn't?

As you finished, did you:

- feel relieved, or sorry it had to end?
- say "Never again!", or sign up for next year?

What did you gain from the experience?

A social worker

Track 5.1

In the student book we met Rose, a social worker in northern Uganda. She loves her work and is obviously dedicated to the community she serves. But how did she become a social worker? Listen to the interview and then select the best answers to the multiple-choice questions that follow. Circle the correct response from A, B, or C.

Check your understanding

1 What is Gerry doing a survey of?

   A jobs in Uganda

   B social work in Uganda

   C social workers in Uganda

2 What was the name of Rose's husband?

   A Watson

   B Gerry

   C we are not told

3 Who is Agnes?

   A a social worker

   B Rose's sister

   C the person interviewing Rose

4 What did Agnes do for Rose?

   A made her panic

   B took her for walks

   C helped her get her life together

5 What did Agnes encourage Rose to become?

   A a self-confident do-it-all

   B a counsellor

   C a teacher

6 Which of these words do you think best describe how Rose felt 11 years ago, after her husband died? Circle all the words you think are appropriate.

happy   sad   excited   miserable   helpless

desperate   hopeful   grateful

7 How would you describe Rose as she is now? Write down as many words and phrases as you can think of in two minutes to describe her and her working life.

An international aid worker

One of the possible jobs involving travel featured in the student book was that of international aid worker. The information given was a very general introduction to what an aid worker might do. What sort of things do you associate with international aid? What is the job actually like?

Building your vocabulary

Check the meaning of the following words and circle the word or phrase that is the closest match. The first one has been done for you.

implemented	completed / (carried out) / understood
affected	altered / made ill / sweet
launched	started / on board ship / eaten
monitor	dragon / control / keep an eye on
set my sights on	shoot at / aim for / look closely at
assignments	road signs / jobs to do / hopes
stability	steadiness / unsteadiness / relief from
stay focused	keep in the picture / keep awake / keep mind on job
complex	facial expression / difficult / involving several different things
passion	something you are really keen about / something you dislike / friend

In the blog that follows, an international aid worker tells us what he does and how he got involved.

How I became an international aid worker: Chiran Livera

What does your job involve?

I am currently based in Senegal, West Africa, organizing emergency operations for the International Federation of Red Cross and Red Crescent Societies (IFRC). When a disaster occurs, I work with that country's national Red Cross or Red Crescent society. We jointly organize how the operation will be implemented, based on the needs of the people affected. I travel to the affected regions of the country and design parts of the operation such as logistics, finances, and human resources.

I also make sure that the National Society has all it needs to carry out the planned activities. Once the operation is launched, I continue to give technical assistance and monitor progress from one of our regional hubs.

What inspired you to take on the job?

I'm from Canada, and I always liked to travel and learn about other cultures. During some trips, both in Canada and elsewhere, I saw how people were affected by disasters and this motivated me to help. The Red Cross has an excellent reputation in disaster response, so I wanted to join this organization.

The neutral and independent work of the Red Cross attracted me – Identify with these qualities, as well as with the organization's other fundamental principles.

What route did you take to your current job?

I joined the Red Cross as a volunteer straight after high school and slowly became involved in disaster response in my community. As time went by, my appetite for working in disasters grew and I continued to train and seek opportunities to work in larger and more complex operations. After a few years working in my community, I set my sights on overseas work and moved on to the headquarters of the Canadian Red Cross.

From there the path led to international assignments, which I've been doing for the last few years. I feel very fortunate to be where I am and it is important to me to always connect with my volunteer roots in the Red Cross, as our work in disaster response is based on this.

What was the biggest challenge in getting where you are today?

Understanding some of the personal sacrifices required to continue on this path. Working in international disasters is a privilege, though it is not easy and certainly not for everyone. It is difficult to maintain stability with friends and family as I'm always on the move and this is a big cost that disaster workers must understand and be comfortable with.

Ultimately, it becomes a lifestyle choice and I have learned to adapt. I have also been fortunate to develop great new friendships along the way and find solutions to staying connected with friends and family.

What advice would you give to an aspiring aid worker?

Stay determined and seek out opportunities wherever they present themselves. Each one builds our strengths and ultimately defines the type of aid worker we become, so it is important to stay focused on where we want to go and seek opportunities related to that. It is not simple to become an aid worker, and it's difficult to stay an aid worker.

I've found that it's important to find a passion in this line of work. For many of us, it is to help people who are affected by a crisis and unable to cope. Aid work can be daunting as there is much to do and the work seems never-ending.

However, staying focused on the ultimate objective and keeping the people we help at the centre of everything we do helps us re-focus and put things in perspective.

Source: adapted from www.blogs.redcross.org.uk/ international/2013/07/how-i-became-an-international- aid-worker-chiran-livera

Check your understanding

1 Where does Chiran come from?

----

2 What first made him want to join the Red Cross?

----

3 What other qualities about the work of the Red Cross attracted him?

----

4 Where did he first work for the Red Cross?

----

5 How does his service as an international aid worker affect his friendships? He mentions one positive and one negative point. What are they?

Positive: --

Negative: --

6* Imagine that you meet Chiran. Write a brief description of what you think he would be like.

Language focus

Reported speech

The piece about Chiran is an example of first-person narrative. He is asked questions, which he answers:

> "What does your job involve?"

> "I am currently based in Senegal …"

However, such accounts are often reported:

> *When Chiran was asked what his job involved, he replied that he was at that time based in Senegal …*

You will notice that the narrative has changed from the first person – "I" – to the third person – "he" – and the present tense has moved into the past. Instead of Chiran speaking now – "I am …" – we are saying what he said then – "he was". Similarly, "currently" refers to the present – now – and has to be changed when reported later.

The simple rules to remember are:

> First person becomes third: "I" = "he" (and "we" = "they")

> Tenses move one stage into the past: "is" = "was" (and so on)

> Time moves from the present: "now" = "then" (and so on)

> Place moves from near to far: "here" = "there" (and so on)

> "I am now here" = "he was then there"

Now try changing these sentences into reported speech:

1 "I come from Canada and work for the Red Cross in Senegal."

----

2 "My family is very understanding and wishes me well."

----

3 "If you want to be an international aid worker, I recommend the Red Cross."

Put these sentences in reported speech into direct speech:

4 He said that he was standing at the spot where the temple had been.

----

5 He considered that working as an aid worker was a privilege.

----

6 They didn't know the answer but fortunately John did, they said.

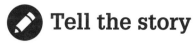 # Tell the story

Imagine that you are Chiran Livera. You are sent on an international
assignment to help clear the site of a recent earthquake and are there for
ten days. Your tasks involve searching damaged buildings, giving first aid
to the injured and helping those who have lost their homes. At the end
of that time you have to file a report. Write an extract from that report, in
which you describe searching the ruins of a building and what you found.

There was one more building a little further away.

As we approached, I _____

A puppeteer

One career that we heard about in the student book was that of puppeteer. Corina Bona is a puppet-maker and performer and, from her early days in Bristol, she has gone on to build a busy and successful career.

Building your vocabulary

Check the meaning of these words and then see if you can complete the crossword below.

projection   atmosphere   enhanced   prestigious   torso   resurgence   mainstream

sculpted   latex   wardrobe mistress   veil

Across

3 lady in charge of costumes in a theatre

7 image cast on to a screen

8 carved into shape

9 what is usual

11 returning powerfully

Down

1 foam rubber

2 body

4 surrounding feeling

5 improved

6 famous or important

10 face covering

Audience participation in puppetry

Gonzoole is one of Corina's latest projects, working with other artists. The performances combine shadow puppetry, live music, and poetry.

Shadow puppetry is created with cut-outs, using front and back projection techniques with a screen. Corina aims to create a warm and supportive atmosphere that encourages audience participation.

"Enabling the audience to create and participate in stories is important to my work. The themes we are developing for Gonzoole are often based around the sea.

"The audience and performers work together to explore myths, fables, and other stories, which are enhanced by sound and imagery. I love the idea of creating something very different in each performance."

Corina works with several prestigious puppet companies, sometimes using other techniques including torso puppetry. She performs with her head covered by a veil, and her legs are connected with the body of the puppet.

Making puppets to order

Corina also makes puppets to order, mostly for other theatre groups. These might be for children's shows such as "The Elves and the Shoemaker" by Pins and Needles Productions or for adult productions like "Tattoo" for Company of Angels. There has been a recent resurgence in the use of puppets in mainstream theatre, which means that Corina's talents are in demand.

"Before I set to work on making the puppets, I always meet with the theatre director to discuss their needs. Together we look at the function of the puppets, the ability of the puppeteers, and, mostly importantly, the budget. I then select appropriate materials, which are often recycled if possible."

A variety of different techniques are used to make the puppets. The body parts may be sculpted in clay, and these are then cast in plaster before a latex mould is made. Foam is widely used, which is carefully shaped before being covered in fabric.

"I design the look of the puppets, which are often made to look like other actors in the production. Choosing colours and fabrics and sewing are all part of the process.

"Depending on the level of collaboration, I might get some assistance with the sewing. The wardrobe mistress for The Elves and the Shoemaker was a great help with this."

Source: adapted from an article in www.creative-choices.co.uk

Check your understanding

1   What does the show "Gonzoole" have in addition to puppetry?

----

2   What is the audience encouraged to do?

----

3   How does a torso puppet work?

----

4   When making puppets for a theatre company, what three things does Corina need to know?

----

5   What did the wardrobe mistress help with for "The Elves and the Shoemaker"?

6* "...I always meet with the theatre director to discuss their needs." What questions do you think she asks them?

💬 Discussion topic

What kind of career are you interested in? Perhaps you have known for a long time exactly what you want to do. On the other hand, you may still have little clear idea. How do you decide? Some of the things to consider might be:

- job satisfaction – *is it worthwhile?*

- personal fulfillment – *how do I make the most of my potential?*

- financial rewards – *how much money will I earn?*

- contribution to society – *what will I be doing for others?*

- enjoyment – *will I like doing it?*

Can you think of other considerations, perhaps to do with:

- family

- resources

- training – *cost in money and time.*

What is most important? How do you decide?

6 Travel and transport

Cycling

Your town has decided that there need to be more bicycle lanes marked out in the streets to encourage people to use pedal power rather than their cars. Think of three things such a scheme would have to include to make you want to use your bike more.

Building your vocabulary

Match the word on the left to its correct definition on the right. The first one has been done for you.

mayor — the person in charge of a town or city

potholes · holes in the road caused by erosion, cold weather or age

pollution · ring (e.g. a bell)

chime · a type of boat on a river or water channel

ferry · noise, fumes, and rubbish which make a place dirtier

Track 6.1

Listen to a cyclist who has been using a new bicycle route for a month, and then answer the questions that follow.

Check your understanding

1   Who opened the new bicycle route?

----

2   How long has it been open?

----

3 What impact has an increased number of cars had on the town?

----

4 What has Ada been able to see for the first time?

----

5 What does Ada want her audience to do?

6* Are you more likely to cycle now you have listened to Ada?

✏ Spreading the word

You need to help Ada spread the word about the new cycle route. Write the text for a poster which can be printed and put up around the town, telling people about the new route and explaining why they need to drive less and cycle more.

--   --

--   --

--   --

--   --

--   --

--   --

--   --

--   --

--   --

--   --

--   --

--   --

--   --

Polar exploration

Moving beyond the place where we live, we can see that there are many wonderful regions to travel to, a few of which are relatively unknown. An example of a place where few people go is the Antarctic.

Building your vocabulary

Check the meaning of these words before using one word in each gap to complete the passage.

altitude   steep   drifts   summit   sledge

As the climber approached the _____ side of the mountain, he took a deep breath; he

knew some had made it, but not all. He left his _____ in the shelter of a small cave and

turned to see some snow _____ on the distant hills. He started climbing. He always knew

the high _____ of the mountaintop would be hard but he kept going and, after six hours,

reached the _____ .

Scott of the Antarctic

 Robert Scott was an explorer, as well as being in the British Navy. Read this diary entry, which he wrote when he was attempting to be in the first group to reach the South Pole.

February 2nd, 1912

9340. R. 16. Temp.: Lunch -19°C, Supper -17°C. We started well on a strong southerly wind. Soon got to a **steep** grade, when the **sledge** overran and upset us one after another. We got off our ski, and pulling on foot had done 9 miles by lunch at 1.30. Started in the afternoon on foot, going very strong. The tracks were drifted over, but the **drifts** formed a sort of causeway along which we pulled. In the afternoon we soon came to a steep slope – the same on which we exchanged sledges on December 28. All went well till, in trying to keep the track at the same time as my feet, on a very slippery surface, I fell on my shoulder. It is horribly sore to-night and another sick person added to our tent – three out of five injured, and the most troublesome surfaces to come. We shall be lucky if we get through without serious injury. Wilson's leg is better, but might easily get bad again, and Evans' fingers.

At the bottom of the slope this afternoon we came on a confused sea of snow ridges. We lost the track. Later, on soft snow, we picked up E. Evans' return track, which we are now following. We have managed to get off 17 miles. The extra food is certainly helping us, but we are getting pretty hungry. The weather is already a little warmer and the **altitude** lower, and only 80 miles or so to Mount Darwin. It is time we were off the **summit** - another four days will see us clear of it. Our bags are getting very wet and we ought to have more sleep.

Source: www.spri.cam.ac.uk/museum/diaries/scottslastexpedition/page/5

Check your understanding

1 What was the temperature at lunchtime?

---

2 How far had they walked by lunch?

---

3 Name one of the injured men.

---

4 How far were they from Mount Darwin?

---

5 What two problems do they have?

6* More than a century later, the Antarctic is still a fierce place to be. Pick out one detail which is still the same today.

How would you like to spend a week working at –40°C? How about several months? Does the longer time change your view? If you could stay for any length of time at either the Arctic or the Antarctic, how long would you stay, and why?

Track 6.2

Now listen to a modern-day Antarctic explorer.

Check your understanding

1 Which subject did he study at university?

---

2 Where did he study for his doctorate in this subject?

---

3 How long was he in the Antarctic for?

---

4 What did he miss when he was in the Antarctic?

----

5 What does he say a good physicist needs?

6* What do you think is the most difficult part of the explorer's job?

Language focus
Relative pronouns

We looked at "which" in the student book, but there some other examples of relative pronouns that we can now consider.

"Which" refers to a noun:

There is the house, which was built by my Uncle Bill.

"Who" refers to a person:

Joel is a man who is very kind-hearted.

"Whom" indicates an indirect object and is preceded by **"to"**:

Tommy Lee is someone to whom everyone gives thanks.

"Whose" refers to a possession or possessor:

Carol is a florist whose flowers are the best in town.

"That" can be used for nouns (objects and people):

This is a book that I have really enjoyed reading.

Add the correct relative clause into these sentences:

1 That is the man _____ umbrella was stolen last week.

2 She is the lady to _____ I wrote a letter.

3 The cat, _____ was lost, was found by a six-year-old girl.

4 The dog _____ was eating a bone is a Dalmatian.

Holidays

We can, these days, travel thousands of miles just to go on holiday. We can go to a tropical island, to the top of a mountain, or even under the ground in a salt mine. How about under the sea, on a diving holiday? How exciting would that be?

Building your vocabulary

Check the meaning of these words.

shoal   shipwreck   cliff   reef   clam   exhilarating

lengths   hooked   pride of place   reminder

Now answer these questions:

1   Which word refers to a group of fish?

----

2   Which word is an underwater shell creature?

----

3   Which word means very exciting?

----

4   Which word refers to a vessel which has been sunk and is sometimes only partly remaining?

----

5   Which word is something to make you remember?

 Track 6.3

Now listen to a diver talking about his life.

Check your understanding

1   How long has Dan been a diver?

----

2 How old was he when he first went on a diving course?

----

3 Where did he go diving a year later?

----

4 What does he say was the best bit about that dive?

----

5 Where has he put the certificate he was given?

6* How would you feel if you went on a dive?

✏️ Diving to shipwrecks

You have always had an interest in shipwrecks and so you were very excited to hear that a group of divers has just discovered one off the local coast. You would like to join them to dive around the shipwreck.

Write an application letter to the person in charge of the shipwreck, asking if you can join them to explore it further.

Which special qualities do you have which will be of particular interest to them?

Flying

Building your vocabulary

stunt-flying   aviation   convictions   conventional   biplane   canary   relented

prank   ticker tape   altitude

Check the meaning of these words before completing the crossword puzzle. Choose one word for each clue.

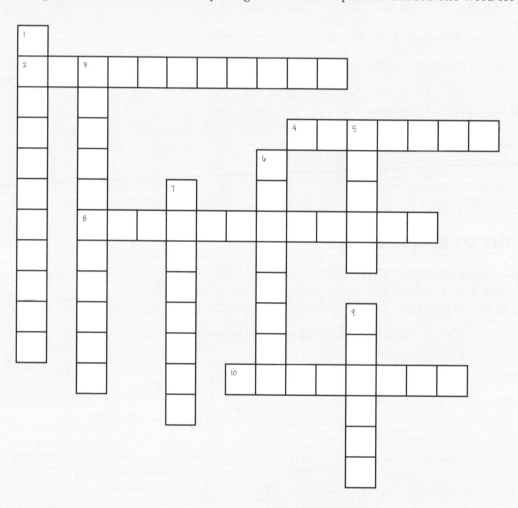

Across

2   A strip of paper upon which information was printed

4   An aeroplane which has two sets of wings, rather than the usual one set

8   Behaving in an accepted normal way

10 Gave in

Down

1   A display in the sky where aeroplanes do tricks

3   Beliefs

5   A joke

6   The height above sea level a person or object is

7   A word which relates to all means of flying

9   A small yellow bird

In the student book, we met a modern-day female pilot who has broken the rules to learn how to fly without the use of her arms. Now read about another ground-breaking pilot.

When 10-year-old Amelia Mary Earhart saw her first plane at a fair, she was not impressed. "It was a thing of rusty wire and wood and looked not at all interesting," she said. It wasn't until Earhart attended a **stunt-flying** exhibition, almost a decade later, that she became seriously interested in **aviation**. A pilot spotted Earhart and her friend, who were watching from an isolated clearing, and dove at them. "I am sure he said to himself, 'Watch me make them run,'" she said. Earhart, who felt a mixture of fear and pleasure, stood her ground. "I believe that little red airplane said something to me as it swished by."

Although Earhart's **convictions** were strong, challenging prejudicial and financial obstacles awaited her. But the former tomboy was no stranger to disapproval or doubt. Defying **conventional** feminine behaviour, the young Earhart climbed trees and hunted rats. She also kept a scrapbook of newspaper clippings about successful women in fields including film direction and production, law, advertising, management, and mechanical engineering.

She left school to work as a nurse's aide and later became a social worker. Earhart took her first flying lesson on January 3, 1921, and in six months managed to save enough money to buy her first plane, a second-hand two-seater **biplane** painted bright yellow. Earhart named the plane **"Canary"** and used it to set her first women's record by rising to an **altitude** of 14,000 feet.

One afternoon in April 1928, a phone call came for Earhart at work. "I'm too busy to answer just now," she said. After hearing that it was important, Earhart **relented**, though at first she thought it was a **prank**. "How would you like to be the first woman to fly the Atlantic?" he asked, to which Earhart promptly replied, "Yes!" She was asked to join pilot Wilmer "Bill" Stultz and co-pilot/mechanic Louis E. "Slim" Gordon. The team left the USA in a plane called Friendship on June 17, 1928, and arrived in Wales approximately 21 hours later. When the crew returned to the United States they were greeted with a **ticker-tape** parade in New York and a reception held by President Calvin Coolidge at the White House.

Today, the world remembers Amelia Earhart for her courage, vision, and groundbreaking achievements, both in aviation and for women. In a letter to her husband, written in case a dangerous flight proved to be her last, this brave spirit was evident. "Please know I am quite aware of the hazards," she said. "I want to do it because I want to do it. Women must try to do things as men have tried. When they fail, their failure must be but a challenge to others."

Source: www.ameliaearhart.com

Check your understanding

1 How did Amelia react when she first saw a plane?

----

2 Name an obstacle which stood in the way of her flying.

----

3 Give one adjective to describe Amelia's first plane.

----

4 When did she and two others leave to cross the Atlantic for the first time?

----

5 Name one thing that happened when they returned to the USA after this flight.

6* How does Amelia view failure?

You are in the middle of flying around the world, solo. Where are you? What have you seen in the last week?

Update your blog to tell your followers what you have been up to.

Well, the last week has been the most incredible of the journey so far

---

⬤ Discussion topic

Your class has been chosen to build a new holiday complex but you need to finalize the plans before they are presented to the funding committee. Plan the details in these groups:

Group One – you will decide where the complex will be and what the accommodation there will be like. Is it going to be a single hotel; a main hotel with smaller blocks around it; small individual houses; or something else?

Group Two – you will decide on the decor of the hotel – in the main areas as well as the individual rooms. First, decide whether they will be complementary, then decide whether all the rooms will be the same or unique. Think about colour, fittings, and the overall look of the rooms.

Group Three – you will decide on the pricing of the rooms – how much it will cost to stay, how this will vary over the year and what promotions you will offer in the first month. You also have to decide where the offers will be available (e.g. the local newspaper) and for how long they will be valid.

Group Four – you will be deciding what food will be available at the complex. What kind of food will the restaurant have on its menu? What other options for food and drink will there be around the holiday complex?

Language focus

Past continuous tense

We saw the past continuous being used in the Student's book to set a scene for a story and for simultaneous action. Here are further examples of each:

- I **was** just **starting** to continue reading my book when there was a knock at the door.

- He **was singing** to himself in the shower when he suddenly remembered who he had seen earlier in the day.

Now, practise putting the verbs into the past continuous, one in each sentence:

1 When she (cook) the dinner, she heard the good news on the radio.

2 It was when he (use) his knife that night that he realised he wanted to be a surgeon.

3 They saw the Milky Way for the first time as they (stand) in the garden of their new house.

4 He (look) for the remote control when he saw a ring on the floor.

5 They sang the beautiful music they (practise) each week this term.

Building your vocabulary

stacked   soared   relic   era

consultant   noughties   cast

Look up these words to make sure you know what they mean. Now add each word into one of the gaps in the text below.

When he first joined the company, the _____ thought

that even the building looked like a _____ from

another _____ and certainly not a company which

was doing well in the _____. He introduced the

main changes in the company until eventually sales

_____ and the product was _____ in

every store. Soon a film about the company was made, famous actors

were _____, and the tag lines they were known for

made the latest version of the English dictionary.

Lego

 Read about Lego, the famous children's toy, and answer the questions that follow.

The plastic bricks and their spin-off toys are possibly the world's favourite toy.

It may not be a language familiar to most, but we all know two Danish words, even if we don't know that we know them. *Leg godt* means play well and it was that

short phrase that gave the name to a small brick which has entertained children and adults for generations.

The company was set up in 1932 by Danish carpenter Ole Kirk Christiansen. About a decade later, the company started making plastic bricks which were self-locking and could be easily **stacked**. They had the ideas of including studs on the bricks, patented this idea in 1958, and used bright colours for the bricks.

In 1961, the first Lego wheel came off the production line. Lego now makes more than 300 million a year, more than Goodyear tyres. Six years later and Duplo was created for preschool children and, in 1978, the mini figure was introduced and sales **soared**. Lego seemed unstoppable right up until the end of the century.

Then things started to go wrong. Cheaper products were more widely available on the market. What had seemed revolutionary in the 1950s had become a **relic** of a past **era**. Lego was being replaced by Nintendos and Xboxes. Despite opening up new stores and designing new kits, sales were slowing and the low point came in 2003 when it was at risk of being sold off.

Then Jorgen Vig Knudstorp entered the company, a young former teacher who had become a **consultant**. Kits which were not making a profit were no longer made and replaced by what Lego had at first been about – having fun building with bricks.

Children of the **noughties** now want to play with Lego and it reminds parents of their own childhoods. Thinking outside the box nearly put Lego out of business. When simple pieces of Lego were put back in the box, they started making money again, with sales of over 23 billion a year.

A new animated movie, with a voice **cast** including Will Ferrell, Liam Neeson, and Morgan Freeman, shows that Lego has a long life ahead of it.

Source: www.sundayexpress.co.uk

Check your understanding

1   What does the Danish phrase *leg godt* mean in English?

----

2   In which year was Lego patented?

----

3   How many tyres does Lego make each year?

----

4   What did Jorgen Vig Knudstorp do before he joined Lego?

----

5   Name a voice actor in the cast of the Lego movie.

6* What trade did Ole Kirk Christiansen have?

What would you change?

Knudstorp changed the future of Lego; what one change would you like to make to your favourite form of entertainment? What are the reasons behind your choice?

🔊 Listening

Watch the well-known singer A.R. Rahman talking about life and his life in the clip, available at the website address given below, and then answer the questions.

www.youtube.com/watch?feature = player_embedded&v = v15g6zU-EG4

Check your understanding

1   According to Rahman, what do you want to try if you have an adventurous nature?

----

2   What did the process help him do?

----

3   What does he want to turn anger into?

----

4   What parts of the elephant did the blind men hold? Give two examples.

----

5   What does he want to see?

6*   Research a song by A.R. Rahman that you like and explain why you like it.

Floella Benjamin

👁 Using your life experiences to help and influence others can be useful, but you don't have to restrict yourself to your blog. Many people have written a full-length book, using their experiences to shape the characters they are writing.

Television presenter Floella Benjamin was born in Trinidad but moved to the UK when she was young. Read this short extract from her novel *Sea of Tears*.

Jasmine's eyes opened and scanned the bare walls of her room. Traces of Blu-tack stained the white wallpaper where her posters had been. Only her bed and a small side-table remained; everything else had gone, even the carpet.

This was the room she had grown up in, the place where she felt happy and secure, the place she ran to when everything was going wrong. Now the shrill beeping of her alarm clock bounced harshly off the bare walls. And the clattering of her mother moving around downstairs was amplified by the emptiness of the house.

Jasmine pulled the duvet over her head and tried to force herself back to sleep but, perfectly on cue, came her mother's yell from the bottom of the stairs.

"Jazzie! It's six o'clock...time to get up. The taxi's here in an hour!"

Jasmine stayed silent. Why did her mother always have to shout so loud?

"Jasmine?"

This time it was her real name. Her Mum always did that. First the pretence at being nice with the Jazzie thing then, when she started to get annoyed, it became Jasmine.

Jasmine went over to the window and pulled aside the old sheet that her mother had put up in place of her lovely, blue, flowery curtains which were now, along with all her other possessions, on their way to Barbados.

Check your understanding

1   Give two examples of items which are still in Jasmine's bedroom.

   ----

2   Why does the alarm clock sound harsher now?

   ----

3   What time is the taxi arriving?

   ----

4   What does her mother call her when she is annoyed?

   ----

5   To which country is Jasmine going?

6* Do you think Jasmine is looking forward to going to Barbados? Why do you think so?

Language focus
Adverbs

The adverbs we choose can affect the way the target reader feels about our writing. Choosing a less common adverb which is synonymous with the one we may have originally thought of may help to broaden the depth as well as the appeal of our writing.

Look at these examples, where the adverb originally thought of can be exchanged for a less common one:

- "Fast" could be replaced by "quickly" or "swiftly".

- Instead of "quickly" you could say "silently" or "noiselessly".

- "Untidily" could be avoided by using "messily" or "chaotically".

By thinking about the range of language we are using, we can make it more interesting.

So where we might have had:

- "The athlete ran quickly."

we can now have:

- "The athlete ran swiftly."

Look at these sentences. Replace the highlighted adverb with one which is synonymous but less common:

1 He played the music very **loudly**. _____

2 Her mother was able to make sponge cakes **perfectly** every time. _____

3 The event was **totally** successful. _____

4 He was **completely** exhausted by the time he had finished the marathon. _____

5 The latest book I have been reading is **extremely** interesting. _____

Pick five adjectives

Sometimes, we have the opportunity in life to repay kindnesses which others have shown us. Watch the following advert and explain your reaction to it. Pick five adjectives to describe it.

www.youtube.com/watch?v = AIpExKZw38k

Richard Whitehead

Some people talk about their life experiences, some use life experiences to help others, while others go out and do something challenging, often to raise money for charity. We have seen entertainers run, sing, act, and play football, all for good causes.

In your student book, we read about Eddie, who ran 43 marathons in 51 days. This was an incredible feat, of course. But what about running 40 marathons in 40 days when your legs stop above your knees (making movement more limited)? That is what the gold-medal-winning UK Paralympian Richard Whitehead has done, running the entire length of the UK from John O'Groats to Land's End.

Read his blog.

Why would anyone run a marathon a day from John O'Groats to Land's End? The answer is simple – to prove that any barrier can be overcome. I'm living proof that having a disability shouldn't stop you from achieving your goals. I'm a strong believer in living a life without limits, what my life has been about is accepting who you are and making the most of it. Once you've done that, you can push the barriers as far as they'll go.

Winning a gold medal at the 2012 Paralympics in London was a stepping stone on this mission and the run is the next stage for me. Hopefully I can pass on a message of hope through my dedication to sport and be an inspiration to all.

✏️ Writing

Write to a national television station asking them to interview Richard. Explain why he should be interviewed and what viewers will find interesting when they see him. Try to include some relevant adverbs in your writing.

Theatre

👁 Going to the theatre has enjoyed a rise in popularity over recent years, but plays need to be increasingly inventive to keep audiences coming back. You read about the musical *The Lion King* in your student book. What is your favourite play or film?

One of the more interesting ways to keep the attention of the audience is to use the idea of a play within a play. Read examples of this technique, which has been used by playwrights and writers for centuries, in the boxes on the right.

A Midsummer Night's Dream

Shakespeare wrote this in the late 16th century and it includes a number of plots. One of the best known is the group of local craftsmen who are rehearsing a play. They encounter several problems, the most famous of which leaves the lead actor with the head of a donkey. The play they rehearse and perform has echoes of the main play itself.

Hamlet

Shakespeare used the same idea in this play, with Hamlet acting out a play in which a king is murdered by his nephew, mirroring the main play. We see the reactions of the actor audience to the play, suggesting how the real audience should react to the main play itself. Chekhov uses *Hamlet* as the play within a play in *The Seagull*.

Noises Off

A web of a play woven by Michael Frayn, this modern piece follows a group of actors rehearsing a play, and we see both the rehearsal and the performance. Intentional confusion sets in and descends into hilarious chaos by the end. This is one of the funniest plays within plays which, unusually, is sustained for the entire length of the play and is not just a short play within another.

Singin' in the Rain

This film moves us from plays within plays to plays within films, where the actors play silent movie stars seeking to increase their popularity in an age when talking movies were first becoming popular.

The French Lieutenant's Woman

More recently, this novel was adapted into a film and shows us two actors who meet while filming a period drama and sees the actors confuse the characters they are playing with their real-life selves.

Check your understanding

1 Which two plays mentioned above were written by the same playwright?

----

2 Which playwright used the work of another playwright?

----

3 In *Hamlet*, we see an audience react to a play but what does it tell us, the other audience?

----

4 Which play has one of the funniest plays within plays?

----

5 In *The French Lieutenant's Woman*, how do the actors meet?

6* Which play would you like to go and see and why?

What do you think?

Imagine you have seen all the plays and films mentioned above. Which do you think is the most interesting play and play within a play?

✏ Writing

Write a review for your school newspaper telling your fellow students which play they should be going to see this term and what makes the play so special.

Track 7.1

The 2012 Olympics and Paralympics were meant to inspire a generation. The people best placed to do exactly that are teachers.

One experience nearly all of us share is the experience of going to school. Looking back on those days has been a source of entertainment for centuries. Playwrights, poets, writers, comedians, and musicians have all looked back at their student days and used them as inspiration for their work.

Alan Bennett's acclaimed play *The History Boys* was later made into a well-received film.

Listen to four students talking about the film of *The History Boys* that they have just seen.

Check your understanding

1 Give an adjective they use to describe the actor playing Hector.

----

2 What does Adi like about the film?

----

3 Why doesn't Dee like it?

----

4 When is the play set?

----

5 How old are the boys in the play?

6* Which teacher has had the greatest influence over you and why?

Make a movie

Watch the movie trailer for the new Lego movie:

www.aboutus.lego.com/en-gb/news-room/2013/june/the-lego-movie-teaser-trailer

Alternative link:

http://www.thelegomovie.com/

The trailer features several well-known figures from the world of entertainment whom Lego has made into figures over the years. There are many novel and TV characters who have not made it to the movies yet – until now.

Choose a story or character you would like to see on the big screen. Write a brief plot outline and decide which actors you would like in your movie, and which music icons you would like to provide the soundtrack to your film.

8 Hobbies and interests

Collectors

Are you a collector? A collector is not just someone who happens to add to piles of possessions by accident, but one who deliberately looks out for things to collect. Collectors take pleasure in looking through their collections and they look after them carefully.

Building your vocabulary

Check the meaning of these words.

pedigree   stashed   indulge   focus   canyons

cartoons   dimension   bolster   unique   depict

Now see if you can use them to fill in the spaces in the sentences below.

1 The shop had a good _____ as the queen herself was one of its customers.

2 The humorous section included _____ drawn by famous artists.

3 He had lots of savings _____ away in a drawer.

4 I photographed the _____ from the air but the picture was not in _____.

5 The painter tried to _____ the scene in a new _____.

6 She used the evening to _____ his confidence.

7 The day was a _____ opportunity to _____ in unusual cakes and sweets.

⊙ How to collect postcards

Deltiology is the official term for collecting (and studying) postcards. The third-largest hobby after collecting stamps and money, collecting postcards can be a very rewarding pastime that can be as broad or as narrow as you'd like, and can be undertaken absolutely anywhere in the world. Even Queen Victoria is thought to have had her own postcard collection, so it's certainly a hobby that has both pedigree and history behind it.

If you're keen to do something with the postcards you've got stashed at home or you're wondering whether or not to indulge in buying them every time you're travelling or sightseeing, perhaps deltiology will open up a new world of collecting for you.

Decide how you will approach collecting postcards. The breadth of postcards is so wide that it's probably a good idea to develop your focus early on to avoid having boxes of unsorted postcards and not knowing what to do with them all. Postcards can be collected in many ways but some of the most common approaches are as follows:

- Postcards by a particular artist
- Postcards from a particular location or country
- Postcards dating from a particular time
- Postcards with a particular theme such as a specific animal like a cat or wildlife, structures such as tall buildings or bridges, natural wonders such as waterfalls or canyons, household items such as teapots, artwork from museum collections, transport such as trains, trams or planes, beach scenes, Valentine's Day, Christmas, Star Trek, etc. (the possibilities are endless)
- Postcards that are humorous or have cartoons on them.

If you have a particular interest, consider collecting postcards related to that interest. For example, if you love horses, then postcards of horses will always appeal to you. All sorts of interests like ballet, rugby, board games, aircraft spotting, museums, dinosaurs, weapons, and food are likely to be found on postcards in one way or another. This can add a very interesting dimension to postcard collecting that will bolster your love of your other interest in a unique way.

- Some people only collect postcards when they travel. Given the great photos that professional photographers can take of a place you're visiting, it can be a good way to ensure that you have at least one really good photo of the place you've visited! It's also helpful to get postcards that depict different seasons or weather from what you're experiencing on your visit.

Source: www.wikihow.com/Collect-Postcards

Check your understanding

1   What does a deltiologist do?

----

2   Many postcard collectors specialize, for example, in postcards by one particular artist. Give one other specialization mentioned.

----

3 If your hobby is aircraft spotting, what does the writer suggest you can do to bolster that interest?

----

4 Why is it a good idea to collect postcards of places you visit on your travels?

----

5 What does the writer suggest you can also look out for in postcards of places you visit?

6* Summarise briefly why you should consider collecting postcards, according to the article.

✏ Your postcard collection

Perhaps you have a postcard collection. Write a brief description of your collection, including a description of your favourite card.

If you don't collect postcards, give a brief description of one that you might begin to build up, maybe based on a special interest you have. What pictures would you look out for? What would be your most prized one?

Language focus

Prepositions

Many of our most common idiomatic expressions, especially in speech, are formed by adding a preposition to a verb. "What time did you get up?" is a simple question about the time your day began. "How did you get on?" is a rather less obvious question about how well you did at something. In the opening paragraph of this workbook chapter, "look out for", "look through" and "look after" are all used. The meaning was probably clear to you. But can you find expressions using the verb "look" plus a preposition (or two) that mean the following?

check a reference	be a spectator (but not take part)	take care of
consider (someone as)	feel superior to	admire
check (for mistakes)	expect	
investigate	beware	

Now see how many idiomatic expressions you can come up with using these verbs:

take   come   run   get   play

 Track 8.1

Listen to the interview in which Renate tells the story of her postcard collection and then answer the multiple-choice questions that follow. In each case select the best answer by circling it.

Check your understanding

1 What relation was Renate to Thora?

  A cousin

  B aunt

  C niece

2 Who did Thora work for?

  A the UN

  B a postcard company

  C a travel company

3 What did Thora ask Renate to do?

  A to keep sending cards

  B to collect cards

  C to make a collection of the cards she sent her

4 How did Thora keep her promise?

  A she sent Renate specially signed cards

  B she changed to sending envelopes instead of cards

  C she stopped sending postcards

5 What did Renate do in memory of her aunt?

  A she travelled the world

  B she continued the collection

  C she married Jacques

Listening to music

Most of us enjoy music of some form. We listen to it to relax, have it on in the background while we do something else or listen for the pleasure of creative sound. Do you ever wonder why? What is there about listening to music that calms us, excites us or helps us escape?

Building your vocabulary

interspersed   fleeting   bizarre   utilitarian   fragment   neurological   shiver   rural

avenues   craniotomy   familiarity

Look up the meaning of these words and then complete the crossword below.

Across

4 found at intervals

6 strange

10 to do with the brain/nervous system

11 being accustomed to something

Down

1 useful or practical

2 momentary

3 ways to something

5 small part

7 surgery on a portion of the skull

8 of the country

9 quiver with delight/cold

⊙ The effect of music

In the online conversation that appears below, Laurens Rademakers asks why music affects us. You can read what he said and how one person replied.

Why does music "touch" us emotionally? It doesn't make sense.

Laurens Rademakers:

This is a profound mystery which I cannot begin to ponder. Perhaps you can help?

Think of it: technically speaking, music is just a collection of sounds interspersed by silence.

But every human being knows of pieces of music that really "touch" him or her emotionally. These emotions can be very strong, and transport you to another "place".

How is it possible that a mere collection of sounds gets associated in our brain with memories, experiences, emotions, stories, images, feelings…? Why can we even cry when hearing a particular piece of music or even a fleeting, short succession of a few notes?

It's totally bizarre. I don't understand. It makes no sense, as far as I can see.

Sense? No, because:

- (Apparently) there's no "utilitarian"/"economic" value to music.

- (Apparently) there's no biological/evolutionary advantage – we are hunters and gatherers, so with some brutally uttered noises we should get by well while hunting mammoths and elephants.

- There seems to be no real social value either (as some music can be too private, and a singular fragment may touch a single person at a strictly single, private moment).

- Maybe there's a neurological advantage (releasing energy in excessively charged neurons, or something to that extent…).

In any case: how can we ever explain the fact that music "touches" us and generates "feelings" that can touch our entire body and make us shiver?

Source: Adapted extract from www.ted.com/ conversations/3796/why_does_music_touch_ us_emot.html

Reply from Colleen Steen

Laurens asks an excellent question for which I do not have the answer…only experiences.

I think there is a social value, because music connects people all over the world. One thing I've noticed while travelling to very rural areas is that original music is very similar in many geographically separated areas of the world.

Music seems to make a connection sometimes when many other avenues fail to make the connection. I've entertained in nursing homes and, very often, residents who do not communicate in any other way will start moving to the beat of the music and often sing along with the words, even though they do not remember their own name or members of their family.

When I was unconscious, after a near fatal head/ brain injury and craniotomy, my daughter had all the tunes I was familiar with plugged into my ears most of the time. Did the familiarity of the music help bring me back to this consciousness? Did it help me to heal from an injury I was not supposed to recover from? We will never know for sure, but it apparently didn't hurt.

Check your understanding

1 What does Laurens Rademakers suggest are the two basic components of music?

----

2 What can be the effect of hearing fragments of music, even only a few notes?

----

3 What other effect does Laurens suggest music can have on your body?

----

4 How does Colleen Steen suggest music helps in nursing homes?

----

5 How had Colleen been helped by music?

6* What examples of music "touching us emotionally" have impressed you in this article and the reply? Explain briefly why you have chosen them.

✎ Join in the conversation

You have read two people's ideas about how music affects our emotions. What do you think? Write your contribution to the conversation.

- Think what music means to you.
- Try to give some examples, perhaps naming a tune that has special memories for you.
- Tell of an occasion when music helped you.
- If music doesn't do much for you, why do you think that might be?

Building your vocabulary

decent	involved and difficult
religiously	adjust to fit
rudiments	thinking about it later
in retrospect	very conscientiously
potential	reasonable
accomplish	possible
gear (verb)	basics
complex	successfully do

Look at the words in the left-hand column and match them to the meanings in the right-hand column. Some of these are a little different from the meanings that you may already be familiar with.

Playing an instrument

 There is nothing quite like playing an instrument yourself. In our next passage a professional drummer gives some tips for would-be drummers and tells us about his own experience.

How do I play the drums?

So, you want to play the drums? I warn you, it takes practice. But if you are enthusiastic about it, and have a halfway decent sense of rhythm, you can get pretty good in no time.

What's the first step? Well, you need to get your hands on a drumset. And maybe you can't afford one right now. So what do you do? Well, I can only speak from my experience, and there were a couple of key things I did early on, before I was able to convince my dad to buy me my first kit.

- Make friends with drummers who already play. Most musicians are only too happy to take a beginner under their wing, or at least show them a thing or two. Secondly, you'll have a chance, if you're nice, to sit down behind their kit and hit a couple of things, see if drumming is really for you. When I first got started, I had a friend who had a drumset set up in his parents' basement. I used to go over there religiously after school, and play beats and compare notes with him. It got my hands on a real drumset long before I could actually buy one of my own.

- If your school has a music programme, and it includes drumming, give it a try. I never really wanted to join the school band, but I did want to practise. In my school there was a rehearsal room with a drumset set up in it; the room was usually empty. I went there a lot, much to the music teacher's annoyance, but after chasing me out of there about a dozen times, he finally gave up, threw his hands up in the air, and let me practise. He tried in vain to get me to learn the rudiments and join the school band, which, in retrospect, would have been a great idea, it would have made me a much better drummer… but I just wanted to learn how to play Led Zeppelin and Aerosmith songs and join a rock band.

Okay, that's the first step… Getting your hands on an actual drumset, so you can get the feel of what it's like to hit the various drums and cymbals.

What's next?

- Learn a very basic beat to play.

- Learn some basic reading skills, so you can learn more beats at your leisure. If you can do that, you're on your way to reading drum music. It's really not that hard.

- You can get drum lessons. I would advise making it very clear to your potential teacher just what you want to accomplish so that the teacher can gear the lessons to your needs.

- Play along to CDs. And don't make the mistake of starting with the hardest, most complex stuff that you know and love. Pick simple songs to start with, so you can get used to the idea that it's all possible for you.

- Oh, and one more thing. Experience can be the best teacher. Good luck!

Source: Adapted extract from www.iplaythedrums.com/howtoplay.htm

Check your understanding

1 What does the writer say you need to be ready to do?

----

2 Where was the drumset that he first played?

----

3 What two things did the school music teacher want him to do?

----

4 What sort of band did he want to play in?

----

5 When you play along to CDs, what kind of music should you first try?

6* "I can only speak from my experience." What else indicates that the writer is speaking from experience?

Why don't you give it a go?

You and your friends are hoping to form a band. But you need a drummer.

Using the ideas in "How do I play the drums?" and adding some of your own, write an article for your school magazine appealing for someone to join you.

Discussion topic

Your school organizes a leisure and hobbies week. The time is to be devoted to activities of your choice. This can either be spent on your own or in groups. What will you do?

- Will you spend the time on a favourite hobby?
- Or will you try something new?
- Perhaps you could divide the time among several activities?
- Perhaps sport is your choice?
- Or do you have other ideas?

Customs and cultures

Childhood

How were you looked after as a young child? Did you have strict rules to obey, or was your upbringing more flexible? How different was the way you were brought up from how your parents were? There have been marked changes in how children are regarded in many societies, perhaps in yours. But there are still cultural differences – in bedtime rules, for example.

Building your vocabulary

Look up the meaning of the words on the left and then see if you can match them to the definitions on the right.

norm	equals
prevalent	encouraging good health
routinely	period of ten years
outsource (verb)	occurrence
phenomenon	widespread
schedule (verb)	pay someone else to do something
variability	what is usual
decade	set a time for
health-promoting	as part of regular practice
peers (noun)	difference

Track 9.1

Listen to the talk about different cultures and childcare and then select the best answer to each of the multiple-choice questions that follow by circling either A, B, or C.

Check your understanding

1 Two of the sleep consultants are based internationally. One lives in both the USA and France. Where does the other one live?

   A Germany

   B Spain

   C Senegal

2 According to the talk, where are late bedtimes for babies quite normal?

   A in the USA

   B in the Western world

   C in parts of Europe and Asia

3 Where do babies in the West tend to sleep?

   A on their own

   B with an aunt

   C with their parents

4 According to the talk, whose job is it to do the childrearing in many Western countries?

   A grandma

   B the baby's parents

   C the extended family

5 But who does the childrearing in many other cultures around the world?

   A the extended family

   B grandma

   C the baby's parents

◉ Cultural Studies: putting baby to bed

Let's take the basic question of putting the baby to bed. The development of regular sleeping habits is something that many parents are anxious to help their babies achieve. How parents handle this varies considerably across cultures. Putting the baby to bed, as such, is a relatively modern phenomenon: for babies in many traditional societies, sleep is something that just occurs wherever the baby happens to be. In a rural Kipsigis community of Kenya that we studied in the 1970s, for example, mothers made no effort to schedule their babies' sleep. Babies were carried around for much of the day, awake or asleep, in carrying cloths on the back of the mother or an older sister. At night, they slept in skin-to-skin contact with their mothers in a small hut where the other younger children also slept.

A far different situation is found in modern societies where babies often have their own bed or their own room, but there is still a great deal of variability in how parents help their babies get to sleep. For more than a decade, we have studied parenting in its cultural context with an international team of colleagues. The Dutch parents in our research generally emphasized the importance of getting plenty of sleep, and they tucked their babies into bed relatively early. In contrast, parents in Spain usually kept their babies and toddlers up later, and they often stayed with them until they fell asleep. We remember showing a video of a Dutch father putting his six-month-old baby to bed at 6:30 p.m. to a group of students at the University of Seville, Spain. "Won't the baby even see anyone until the next morning?" they asked. What seemed to be a health-promoting practice to the Dutch parents was seen as too emotionally and physically distant to their Spanish peers.

As these examples illustrate, even basic functions such as sleep are culturally structured, providing different developmental experiences for children across cultures.

Source: Adapted extract from www.sgiquarterly.org/ essay2009Jan-1.html

Check your understanding

Instead of answering a set of questions checking your understanding of the passage you have just read, you are going to be setting the questions! Reread the passage carefully and prepare five questions to put to others in your class. Begin by noting down the main points in the passage. Once you have done this, select five and turn them into questions. Remember the following:

- Keep the questions simple – *they are meant to help understanding, not to catch people out.*

- Make sure the answer to each question is actually in the passage – *they are not a test of knowledge of the subject, but of understanding of the passage.*

- Answers don't have to be evenly spaced through the passage – *some paragraphs will be more informative than others.*

- Questions should usually be asked in the order the answers appear in the passage – *if a question is out of sequence, say so and explain briefly why.*

- Always try to be specific – *avoid vague questions, for example, "What are Dutch parents like?"*

Interview time

Suppose that one of the baby-rearing consultants comes to your school to interview students about childrearing practices in your culture. The consultant will want to know what usually happens in the upbringing of babies and young children. You are one of the students selected to answer their questions. Think about how you would you answer questions about:

● the time babies are usually put to bed

● where they sleep

● who looks after them

● the extent to which other family members might be involved

● any other relevant information about childrearing in your culture.

Language focus

Emotive writing

In the student book we saw how two writers observing the same incident can give opposite impressions of what took place, simply by the descriptive language they choose. One man's heroic bravery is another's foolish behaviour. The technical term for this kind of writing, where the writer's opinion is given through the choice of vocabulary, is emotive writing. The facts are sometimes hard to find in the midst of the emotive opinions expressed. Look at these two sentences:

● The home team played superbly, denying their overrated opponents the freedom to play, and were unlucky to lose a close game.

● The visiting side was far superior to their ragged opponents, whose foul play and time-wasting couldn't prevent them losing heavily.

The only facts are that two sides played each other and the visiting side won. Everything else is opinion.

Identify the facts contained in each of the following sentences:

1 My favourite ice cream is a superb mixture of crunchy nuts and cool peppermint.

2 My old-fashioned parents found the friendly welcome of my boyfriend's family embarrassing.

3 The children were carefully nurtured by their devoted grandparents.

4 At 16 years old the boys were forced to undergo a series of stupid rituals to prove they had become adults.

5 The exams were horribly unfair so I didn't quite make it through.

Weddings in different cultures

In the student book wedding customs in several different cultures were featured, especially those relating to traditional Chinese culture. How did they compare with wedding customs in your culture? Which did you find the most unusual? Another culture that has distinct marriage customs is described below.

Building your vocabulary

Look up the meaning of these words and see if you can complete the crossword below.

prosperity   bouquets   fertility   felicity   colleagues   determined   pinning   substitute

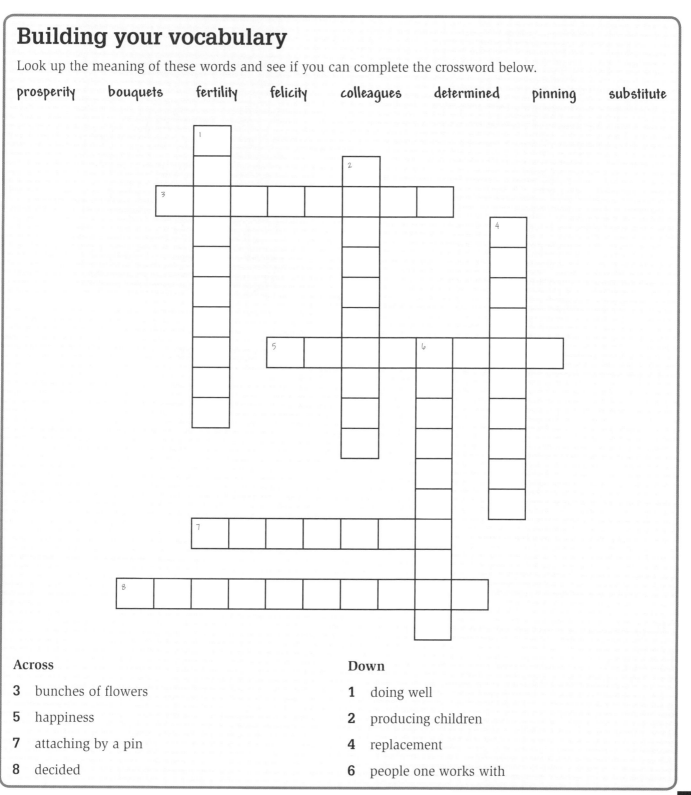

Across

3 bunches of flowers

5 happiness

7 attaching by a pin

8 decided

Down

1 doing well

2 producing children

4 replacement

6 people one works with

Two or three days before the wedding, the couple organizes a celebration called *Krevati* (Greek for bed) in their new home. In Krevati, friends and relatives of the couple put money and young children on the couple's new bed for prosperity and fertility in their life. After the custom, they usually have a party with food and music.

On the day of the wedding the groom cannot see the bride until the wedding ceremony. The groom usually arrives first in church and waits for the bride, who usually arrives late. After they exchange flower bouquets, they have the wedding ceremony, where the best man puts the wedding rings and crowns on the couple. At the end of the wedding ceremony, as the newly wedded pair leave the church, the guests throw rice and flowers for fertility and felicity. Special guests, such as close friends and family, receive sugar-coated almonds (traditionally an odd number, usually seven but sometimes five) as a gift from the couple.

After the ceremony, usually the couple hold a great wedding party in some place with plenty of food, drinks, music, and dance, usually until the next morning. The wedding party starts with the invited people waiting for the couple, who usually come after. They start the dancing and eventually eat a piece of their wedding cake. At some point during the party, they also dance the traditional *zeibekiko* (groom) and *çiftetelli* (bride).

A typical Greek wedding will usually have more than 100 invited people (but usually 250–500) who are friends, siblings, grandparents, uncles, aunts, first or second cousins, neighbours, and colleagues. It is common to have guests whom the couple has never met before. This is because the people who will be invited are usually determined by the parents of the couple and not by

Example of the traditional "money dance" at a Greek wedding

the couple themselves. Traditionally, the whole village would have attended the wedding, so very often the parents invite friends of theirs, and their children, to the weddings of their own children.

There are many other traditions which are local to their regional areas. One famous tradition is the pinning of money on the bride's dress. This custom originated in one part of Greece as a substitute for wedding presents, and it has become more widespread recently.

Source: Adapted extract from www.en.wikipedia.org/ wiki/Wedding_customs_by_country

Check your understanding

1 What two things are put on the couple's bed in the celebrations a few days before the wedding?

----

2 What do these symbolize?

----

3 What do the bride and groom give each other immediately before the marriage ceremony?

----

4 What is thrown over the couple as they leave the church?

----

5 What is given to special guests at the ceremony?

6* Which custom described here do you find the most unusual? Explain why.

Greek wedding video

Watch the video of highlights of a Greek wedding available at www.youtube.com/watch?v = t4RfNujogRA. How many of the customs referred to in the earlier passage about Greek marriage customs can you spot? Make a note of each one and of any other unusual points that you notice.

At a Greek wedding

Imagine that you were a guest at that Greek wedding. Send an email to a friend telling them all about it. Begin with "I went to my Greek friend's wedding yesterday. It was really different …"

_____

_____

_____

_____

_____

_____

_____

_____

_____

_____

_____

Key skills

Further punctuation practice

In the student book the importance of correct punctuation was noted. Here are some more sentences that require punctuation to make their meanings clear:

1 our friend spyroulla married george at a greek wedding said suki

2 where was it held i asked

3 in birmingham she replied i was one of the guests

4 lucky you i said i never get invited to anything

5 poor you said suki when i get married ill let you come

6 youre too kind i said i shall look forward to that day

7 me too she replied they made a lovely pair

8 who did i don't know who youre talking about

9 george and spyroulla of course their wedding was special

10 you can see it on the video she added

Caring for the dead

Death is something we seldom think about, although it comes to us all. But how we deal with it varies considerably from one culture to another, as was explored in the student book, where some unusual examples of how different cultures, past and present, help communities to dispose of their dead. Two more are described here.

Building your vocabulary

entourage	burial
lamas	flesh-eating animals
flanked	follow
yurt	nourishment
predators	Mongolian or Tibetan priests
karma	a central Asian tent
ensue	cut into pieces
dismembered	group of attendants
sustenance	to have alongside
interment	distinctive atmosphere

Look up the meaning of the words on the left and then see if you can match them to the definitions on the right.

Practices in Asia

Air sacrifice – Mongolia

Lamas direct the entire ceremony, with their number determined by the social standing of the deceased. They decide the direction in which the entourage will travel with the body and they choose the specific day and time when the ceremony can happen.

Mongolians believe in the return of the soul. Therefore the lamas pray and offer food to keep evil spirits away and to protect the remaining family. They also place blue stones in the dead person's bed to prevent evil spirits from entering it.

No one but a lama is allowed to touch the corpse, and a white silk veil is placed over the face. The naked body is flanked by men on the right side of the yurt while women are placed on the left. The family burns incense and leaves food out to feed all visiting spirits. When the time comes to remove the body, it must be passed through a window or a hole cut in the wall to prevent evil from slipping in while the door is open.

The body is taken away from the village and laid on the open ground. A stone outline is placed around it, and then the village dogs that have been penned up and not fed for days are released to consume the remains. What is left goes to the local predators.

The stone outline remains as a reminder of the person. If any step of the ceremony is left out, no matter how trivial, bad karma is believed to ensue.

Sky burial – Tibet

This is similar to the Mongolian ceremony. The deceased is dismembered by a rogyapa, or body breaker, and left outside away from any occupied dwellings, to be consumed by nature.

To the Western mind this may seem barbaric, as it did to the Chinese who outlawed the practice after taking control of the country in the 1950s. But, in Buddhist Tibet, it makes perfect sense. The ceremony represents the perfect Buddhist act, known as Jhator. The worthless body provides sustenance to the birds of prey that are the primary consumers of its flesh.

To a Buddhist, the body is but an empty shell, worthless after the spirit has departed. Most of the country is surrounded by snowy peaks, and the ground is too solid for traditional earth interment. Likewise, it is mostly above the tree line, so there is not enough fuel for cremation.

Source: Adapted extract from www.matadornetwork. com/bnt/10-extraordinary-burial-ceremonies-from-around-the-world

Check your understanding

1   In Mongolia who is in charge of the funeral arrangements?

----

2   Why are stones put in the dead person's bed?

----

3   How is the body removed from the yurt?

----

4   What is the result of any omission from the ceremony?

----

5   What is left as a reminder of the dead person?

6* What do you find most unusual in the Mongolian and the Tibetan ceremonies?

Discussion topic

We often think of culture as something from the past and of course it is true that many customs throughout the world have their origins in the past, as examples in this chapter have shown. But what about contemporary culture? This is how we live now, the things we do, what we enjoy, and what we value. Consider the following:

* music
* entertainment
* sport
* clothing
* family
* friends
* education
* religion.

What would you identify as the important things in your contemporary culture? How do they differ from those of previous generations? What things do you think will last?

10 The past and the future

Life in the past

What advice would you give to a friend who was feeling depressed? Read about life 100 years ago, perhaps. That is bound to cheer you up; everything is so much better today. One hundred years ago no one had the time to get depressed, did they? They were all too busy struggling to survive till the next (shared) bath or half-day off. But our ancestors did have times when they felt "in low spirits", as they called it. Sydney Smith, writing to a friend in 1820 who suffered from low spirits, offered some interesting advice.

Building your vocabulary

Look up the meaning of the words on the left and then see if you can match them to their definitions on the right.

prescriptions	sadness
acquaintances	overly emotional
dignified	reasonable
concealment	underestimate the value/importance of
melancholy	respectful
sentimental	hiding
benevolence	tiredness
endeavour	casual friends
fatigue	instructions for (medical) treatment
underrate	try
rational	kindness

As the letter was written 200 years ago, there are some words that are used differently or have slightly different meanings from today. To help your understanding some of these are listed below with their present day equivalent:

sensation	feeling
attend to	do something about
lot	situation in life
dramatic representations	plays
excite	arouse
degree	position in society
commonly	usually/habitually
gay	bright
by little and little	little by little/gradually
devoted servant	loyal friend

◉ Letter to Georgiana Morpeth, 16 February 1820

Dear Georgiana,

Nobody has suffered more from low spirits than I have—so I feel for you. Here are my prescriptions.

1st Live as well as you dare.

2nd Go into the shower-bath with a small quantity of water at a temperature low enough to give you a slight sensation of cold.

3rd Amusing books.

4th Short views of human life—not further than dinner or tea.

5th Be as busy as you can.

6th See as much as you can of those friends who respect and like you.

7th And of those acquaintances who amuse you.

8th Make no secret of low spirits to your friends, but talk of them freely— they are always worse for dignified concealment.

9th Attend to the effects tea and coffee produce upon you.

10th Compare your lot with that of other people.

11th Don't expect too much from human life—a sorry business at the best.

12th Avoid poetry, dramatic representations (except comedy), music, serious novels, melancholy sentimental people, and every thing likely to excite feeling or emotion not ending in active benevolence.

13th Do good, and endeavour to please everybody of every degree.

14th Be as much as you can in the open air without fatigue.

15th Make the room where you commonly sit, gay and pleasant.

16th Struggle by little and little against idleness.

17th Don't be too severe upon yourself, or underrate yourself, but do yourself justice.

18th Keep good blazing fires.

19th Be firm and constant in the exercise of rational religion.

20th Believe me, dear Georgiana, your devoted servant, Sydney Smith

Check your understanding

1 Why does Sydney Smith feel sympathy for Georgiana?

----

2 He recommends taking a bath. How warm should the water be?

----

3 How much should she tell her friends about her feelings of depression?

----

4 What drinks does he suggest she should be careful of?

----

5 He suggests that she avoid plays unless they are what?

6* "Live as well as you dare." From what he goes on to say, what do you think Sydney Smith means by "living well"? Give examples.

💬 Questions for Georgiana

Supposing you met Georgiana Morpeth. What questions would you ask her? Remember that it is 1820.

🖊 Email to a friend

You hear that a friend of yours is feeling depressed. Write an email in which you list your "prescriptions" for them, ten things that you suggest will raise their spirits. How does your list compare with that of Sydney Smith?

--   --

--   --

--   --

--   --

--   --

--   --

--   --

Language focus

Past and present tenses

Here is some further practice for you in changing tenses.

To practise using the past tense, try changing the following paragraph from the present tense into the past.

> I live in London and travel by underground every day to the British Museum where I work. I am based in the Ancient Egyptian rooms and am always amazed at the details of daily life in that ancient civilization that have been preserved in the relics on display. My favourite exhibit is the Rosetta Stone. It was such an important discovery because it opened up the way for scholars to read and translate what is written in hieroglyphics. I am responsible for the security and safety of exhibits, some of which have been around for thousands of years. I am learning to decipher inscriptions and am beginning to understand how to go about dating them. It is a wonderful job, I think.

Now try and put it into the future tense.

Ancient Egypt

Below is a continuation of the extract about life several thousand years
ago in Ancient Egypt on page 11 of the student book.

Building your vocabulary

braided   amulets   pendants   kilt   loin cloths   nude   sequins

Look up the meaning of these words. They are all to do with what the Ancient Egyptians wore.

See if you can fit them into the spaces in the sentences that follow.

1   The children wore no clothes but went around _____ .

2   Their hair was plaited or _____ .

3   The _____ sown on to their tunics flashed brightly in the sun.

4   The short skirt, or _____ , came to just above the knee.

5   The _____ worn round their necks were lucky charms or _____ .

6   _____ _____ were worn round the waist by the men working in the fields.

⊙ Egypt: daily life and family life (continued)

Hair

Hairstyles were very similar to those of today. The common folk wore their hair short. Young girls usually kept their hair in pigtails while boys had shaved heads, except for one braided lock worn to one side. Wigs were worn by both men and women. The wigs were made of sheep's wool or human hair, for decoration and for protection from the heat. Wigs were usually worn at parties and official functions. Hair pieces were also added to real hair to enhance it. When not in use, wigs were stored in special boxes on a stand inside the home.

Jewellery

Everyone in Egypt wore some type of jewellery. Rings and amulets were especially worn to ward off evil spirits and injury. Both men and women wore pierced earrings, armlets, bracelets, and anklets. The rich wore jewelled or beaded collars called wesekh, necklaces, and pendants. For the rich, jewellery was made of gold, silver, or

electrum (gold mixed with silver) and inlaid with semi-precious stones of turquoise, lapis lazuli (a deep blue stone), and carnelian (a copper or reddish-orange stone). The poorer people wore jewellery that was made of copper or faience (made by heating powdered quartz).

Clothing

Egyptian clothing styles did not change much throughout ancient times. Clothes were usually made of linens ranging from coarse to fine texture. During the Old and Middle kingdoms, men usually wore a short skirt called a kilt. Women wore a straight-fitting dress held up by straps. The wealthy men wore pleated kilts, and the older men wore a longer kilt. When doing hard work, men wore a loin cloth, and women wore a short skirt. Children usually ran around nude during the summer months, while in the winter, wraps and cloaks were worn. Noblewomen sometimes wore beaded dresses.

During the New Kingdom, noblemen would sometimes wear a long robe over their kilt, while the women wore long pleated dresses with a shawl. Some kings and queens wore decorative ceremonial clothing with feathers and sequins. Most people went barefoot, but wore sandals on special occasions. The king wore very elaborately decorated sandals, and sometimes decorative gloves on his hands. Clothing styles were chosen for comfort in the hot, dry climate of Egypt.

Source: Adapted extract from *Splendors of Ancient Egypt Educational Guide*

Check your understanding

1   Why were wigs worn? Give two reasons.

----

2   What other hair decoration was worn?

----

3   On what parts of the body did they wear jewellery?

----

4   What cloth was usually used to make their clothes?

----

5   What was everyday footwear for most?

6* How were the rich and noble identified by what they wore?

Life in the future

Building your vocabulary

Look up the following words. They will appear in the talk you are about to hear.

wizard   crystal ball gazing   optimistic   utilizing   fossil fuels

biodegradable   debris   composite   squabbling   instilling

Across

2 made up of different things

3 quarrelling

7 establishing an idea in

8 looking into the future

9 waste

10 making use of

Down

1 capable of being broken down into its base components

4 magician

5 e.g. coal, oil

6 not pessimistic

Track 10.1

Listen to the talk "What the world may look like in 100 years" and then answer the multiple-choice questions, circling the answer that you think is the best fit.

Check your understanding

1 What encourages the speaker to think that he might be able to "predict" the future?

   A he is a wizard

   B it has been done by others in the past

   C he has a crystal ball

2 What kind of fuel does he think will be used in 100 years' time?

   A clean

   B fossil

   C none, it won't be needed

3 What does he think cars will run on?

   A plastic

   B water

   C there won't be any cars, just air travel

4 How does he think houses may be heated?

   A with water

   B by their own generated heat

   C they won't need to be heated

5 What does he think the top superpowers will be?

   A China, India, and Russia

   B China, India, and the USA

   C China, India, and Brazil

Do you agree?

What do you think of the suggestions in that talk? Take just three of the things that he makes predictions about – cars, houses and the superpowers – and make notes about your own suggestions for what these might be like in 100 years.

Cars

- Will we still have cars? If not, what might have replaced them?

- What fuel might they use? Can you think of a completely new form of energy?

- What will they look like? You might like to draw one.

Houses

- What will they be like? You might like to do another drawing perhaps.

- What sort of gadgets might they have?

- Where will the power come from? Don't just repeat what you suggested above.

Superpowers

- Which nations will they be?

- Are there any surprise omissions?

- What do you think might be the superpowers' main concerns?

--- ---

--- ---

--- ---

--- ---

--- ---

--- ---

--- ---

--- ---

Track 10.2

Imagine that you have been transported 100 years into the future.
Listen to an extract from an antiques show broadcast in 2115 and then answer the questions that follow.

Check your understanding

1   What two things have replaced boiling a kettle to obtain hot water?

----

2   Where does Amit say electronic readers can still be found in 2115?

----

3 What has replaced them in 2115?

----

4 What exactly is the object from the past that Mia introduces?

----

5 What two uses did this object have, according to Mia?

6* What question would you like to ask Sally, Amit or Mia? What might be their reply?

🗨 Discussion topic

What everyday objects do you think will be out of date and forgotten about in 100 years' time? There have been various suggestions in this chapter, both in the student book and in the pieces we have listened to. Consider three areas of everyday life: in the home, at school or the workplace, and in leisure activities. For each of these, come up with ideas for what is going to disappear.

- **In the home** – What things that we take for granted now may no longer be in use?

- **At school** – Will there still be schools in 100 years? What might they be like? What will be missing?

  Or the workplace – What will have changed and what will be lost as a result?

- **In leisure activities** – How might we be spending our free time? What will have gone?

Compile a list of bygones for 2115 from these three areas. Choose your favourite to describe to someone who has never seen it.

- Be imaginative – what would be the biggest surprise?

- Be original – think of things important to you that will disappear.

- Keep it simple – sometimes it is the most obvious things that are overlooked.

- Have fun!

Communication

 Every picture tells a story

We don't need thousands or even hundreds of words to communicate a message. Sometimes, of course, we need no words at all.

The story of Icarus, the boy who tried to fly towards the Sun, is a well-known one. Somehow, however, the painting of the story by Pieter Breughel the Elder summarizes the story more vividly than any words could. We see not only Icarus falling into the sea, but also ordinary people going on with their lives, not seeing the terrible event happening so close to them.

Can you describe the painting?

 Writing

You have been to a famous museum today and seen your favourite painting. Update your blog by writing about the painting, including the story it depicts. What is it communicating?

My photo

You have just read about a new photography competition in your favourite magazine. The title of the photo has to be "A photo that says a thousand words". You are going to enter the competition as the prize is a year's subscription to the magazine, as well as the latest high-tech digital camera on the market. What are you going to take a photo of, and why?

 ## Listening

We don't need pictures to communicate without words. In the student book we learned how chimpanzees communicate. Watch the clip of Kanzi the bonobo demonstrating how he can respond to his handler's requests.

www.youtube.com/watch?v = 2Dhc2zePJFE

Track 11.1
Now listen to Dr Sue Savage-Rumbaugh, Kanzi's main handler, giving a talk about Kanzi and her work at the Great Ape Trust.

Check your understanding

1 What started Kanzi's interest in fire?

----

2 What did Kanzi learn about fire from the film?

----

3 Why was this new skill interesting to the scientists?

----

4 Why does Kanzi not need fire?

----

5 What does Kanzi use fire for?

6* Which skill would you teach Kanzi if you had the chance?

Language focus

Formal and informal language

When we are communicating, we need to choose our words carefully so the person or people we are talking to are clear about what we wish to tell them. Sometimes we need to use formal language, and at others we need to use less formal language. Put the following types of writing into the correct circle:

speech   blog   article in a newspaper

text message   letter to your boss

tweet   essay in an examination

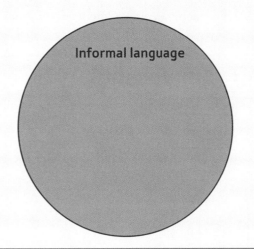

Formal language   **Informal language**

Building your vocabulary

Look up the words on the left and then match them to the correct definition on the right.

pride	proper, formal way of behaving at work
professionalism	most important
key	pleasure
hesitated	direction
trend	paused
turnover	amount of money spent on products

Track 11.2

Listen to the speech by a company director on the importance of communication.

Check your understanding

1   What is the name of the company?

----

2   What does the company pride itself on? Give one example.

----

3   What does the speaker say is a main factor in the company's success?

----

4   Over what period have customer relations improved?

----

5   What will the employees get if they sell more products?

6* Why is this a good company to work for?

Speaking of adverts

Adverts pop up all the time when we are online but what attracts you to an advert? What would make you click on it for more information? Use some of the words in the bubbles to help you.

Look at the advert on this page and decide what it is that the advertisers are trying to communicate.

Advertisers can make up single words to make their advert stand out. Sometimes, however, people decide a few words are not enough and they make up entire languages.

jingle

logo

tag line

celebrity

famous photographer

Building your vocabulary

adopted   strict   version   poverty   incurable

specialize   determined   register

Look up the words and then use them to answer the crossword clues below.

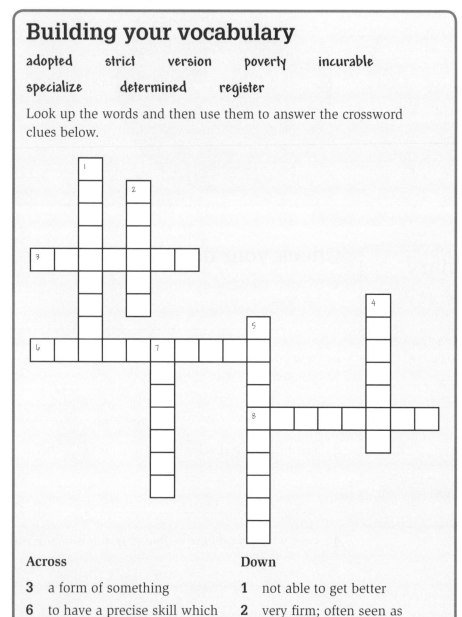

Across

3 a form of something

6 to have a precise skill which one is very good at

8 a list with names to record information about those people

Down

1 not able to get better

2 very firm; often seen as being too firm

4 lack of money

5 having a firm and fixed purpose or reason

7 taken as one's own

◎ Esperanto

Read about Dr Ludovic Zamenhof below and why he created the language of Esperanto.

Check your understanding

1 Why did Esperanto users choose 15 December as a day to celebrate their language?

----

2 How old was Zamenhof when he and his family moved to Warsaw?

----

3 Why did he think a new language should be learned by everyone?

----

4 Who did he try out the new language with at first?

----

5 Why did he keep a register of Esperanto users?

6* Which language you do not know would you most like to learn and why?

The Zamenhof story

Many Esperanto speakers celebrate 15 December, often by giving each other books in Esperanto as presents, because that is the date on which Lazarus Zamenhof was born, in 1859. Lazarus, who later also adopted the name Ludovic, was the person who eventually created Esperanto.

Lazarus lived in a small wooden house in Bialystok, a town which is now in Poland. His father, Marcus, was a teacher of languages and very strict; his mother, Rosalie, was a kind and loving mother to Lazarus and his eight brothers and sisters.

When Lazarus was 14, the Zamenhof family moved to Warsaw, and he went to secondary school there. He was learning more languages by now, but still had his idea about one language for all mankind. He decided that this language would have to be a new language that did not belong to any nation or country, so that it would be fair for everyone – if everyone learned just this one language, as well as their own, they would then be able to talk to each other. By the time he was 19, he had already worked out a version of his international language, which he used with some of his school friends and his brother

Felix. The language worked, and he even wrote some poems in it.

When Lazarus was 25, he began work as a doctor in a small town in Lithuania. He was very upset by the poverty he saw, and by the number of incurable patients that he tried to treat. He decided that this work was too difficult for him, and he began to specialize in treating people's eyes.

All the time that Lazarus was studying and trying to make a success of his career, he kept up his work on his language project, often working until late into the night. He was determined to create a language that would be easier to learn and use than the national languages, and he produced many versions before he came up with his best solution.

Lazarus obtained enough money to have the first book in Esperanto printed and published. It was really a small booklet teaching the reader the basics of the language and giving some examples of how to use it. It also invited students to add their names to a register which Lazarus kept, so that Esperanto users could be introduced to each other.

Source: From www.esperanto.org.uk

Saying what we mean

Of course, what we say is not always what we mean. Look at these three dialogue extracts and decide what speaker A is really trying to say. Choose from these suggestions:

* *It's horrible!*   *Can we stop?*   *I'd like a drink*

1   A: Do you need a break from driving?

    B: No, I'm fine.

2   A: Do you fancy a cup of tea?

    B: No thanks.

3   B: What do you think of this dress?

    A: It's fine.

Track 11.3

Now, listen to two friends talking. There are five extracts of dialogue. For each one, write down what the person speaking last in each extract is really saying.

1   ---

2   ---

3   ---

4   ---

5   ---

Sometimes, it is better to be clearer in what you say, although we often go for the less clear conversation if we feel we need to spare the feelings of our friends.

Discussion topic

You have the chance to introduce a new word into English, the global lingua franca. New words are often nouns which can then be used as a verb.

Think of a new product or trend and then tweet about it, making sure you use the new word. You could use it as a noun before then using it as a verb for greater effect.

How quickly can you get people to understand your new word, and then use it themselves to others?

Global issues

Global brands

Which global brands did you play with as a child? You were perhaps unaware at the time of the extent to which these brands dominated the world. Complete the bubbles to show how one company, Disney, has a presence in many different areas.

Using global brands to learn

Many people these days use a DVD or tablet featuring a favourite character for play and for learning, while others go to the other extreme and use no stimulus other than their own imagination.

Write an email to your local newspaper explaining whether you feel using an electronic product produced by a global brand can be beneficial or whether you believe a more traditional approach to learning is the better way.

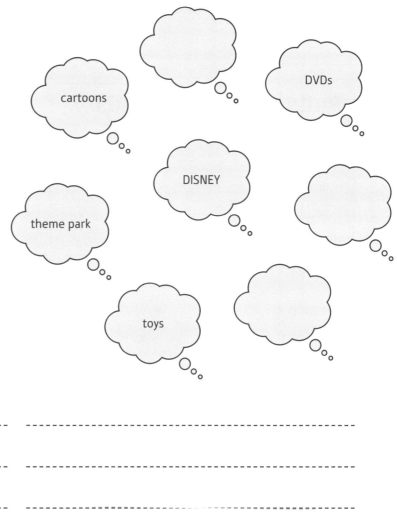

Better brands

Global brands have had to become more ethical in their working practices, often as the result of a campaign in the media. Sometimes, even a lone voice speaking out against a global brand can be enough to halt something.

Tesco found guilty of price-fixing strawberries

McDonalds super-sized me

Starbucks criticized for paying no tax

Building your vocabulary

prioritized	planned way
cited	not having anything in common
mutually exclusive	made the most important
cynical	quoted
intentions	related
associated	something used in place of something else unavailable
assurances	taking a sceptical or negative view
substantial	how something or someone is seen
substitute	considerable
reputation	guarantees

Look up the word or phrase on the left and match it to the correct definition on the right.

◉ Reading

The race to be ethical used to be clearly led by "born-green" companies – organizations that from day one prioritized corporate social responsibility (CSR) in their supply chains.

Lush, the UK-based handmade cosmetics firm, is one such company. Founded in 1995, it now has over 800 stores worldwide, uses factories in more than 40 countries and saw sales of £321 million in 2010/11. It's no surprise that Lush is often cited as an example of why ethical supply chains and financial success aren't mutually exclusive.

In contrast, larger corporations have a much harder time convincing a cynical public that their social and environmental credentials haven't been lifted off the back of the nearest bandwagon. Even with the best of intentions, the sheer size of a major corporation's supplier network – sometimes involving thousands of suppliers – makes it hard for them to make quick, effective and transparent improvements.

Lush calls its supply chain approach "creative buying", where a business looks beyond lowest price and bottom line, and instead buys the best, safest, and most suitable products in accordance with their ethics.

To do this, companies can't only look at what they buy and the associated cost. They need to also be comfortable with those from whom they buy. Organizations should seek assurances that their suppliers are also firms with an ethically sound policy which allows a level of trust to be built into the supply chain for both the purchaser and supplier.

When an organization gets things right, the rewards can be substantial. For example, in 2010 PepsiCo uncovered over $60 million in energy-saving opportunities as a result of a carbon management and energy assessment programme it undertook with its suppliers.

SunChips, a US crisp manufacturer, had to withdraw most of its environmentally sound packaging just 18 months after launch as customers complained about the new noisy bags and sales dropped by 11%. For most of its products, non-recyclable bags were brought back. Consumers often want green as an added value to what they are buying, not as a substitute for something else (in this case a quiet crisp packet).

The Internet and social media leave almost no dark rocks for corporations to hide under. Supply chains and their ethics are firmly in the spotlight and will rightly remain so. Those firms that water the shoots of green growth we've seen in recent years will be amply rewarded, not only in reputation but also on the balance sheet.

Tom Seal is head of research at Procurement Leaders Network.

Source: From www.theguardian.com/sustainable-business/sustainable-supply-chains-ethics-profits?INTCMP=ILCNETTXT3487

Check your understanding

1   What have "born-green" companies made their most important policy?

----

2   How many stores worldwide does Lush have?

----

3   Give two adjectives to describe the products Lush buys in accordance with its ethics.

----

4   How much did Pepsi save as a result of carbon management?

----

5   Why did SunChips cease to use environmentally sound packaging?

6* What is more important to you and why – ethical brand or cheap brand?

Helping the environment

Track 12.1

Listen to Jennifer giving advice on how to get things for free.

Check your understanding

1 What does Jennifer say can be discouraging?

----

2 What is the name of the website Jennifer recommends?

----

3 Give two examples of what you can do on the website.

----

4 What information do you need to include so that people know where you live?

----

5 Give two examples of items that may be found on the website.

6* Which item on the freecycle website interests you most and why?

The Center for 21st Century Energy

Vision

The Center for 21st Century Energy develops technologies for a sustainable energy future, expanding energy resources and reducing carbon dioxide emissions. We are reducing the carbon intensity and expanding the use of renewable energy.

Mission statement

Our mission is to educate the next generation of leaders in energy, science and technology through a world-class program of fundamental and applied research. Our research is developing new energy technologies with significantly better efficiency and lower environmental impacts.

Current focus areas

SOLAR ENERGY: We have developed significant programs in solar energy. New approaches to the design and manufacture of solar cells to reduce their cost are an important area of focus.

WIND ENERGY: Energy generated from floating offshore wind farms is the next frontier in wind energy. Innovative and economical wind turbine floaters are being developed for deployment in large-scale offshore wind farms in water depths up to several hundred meters.

CARBON CAPTURE: More than 85 per cent of our energy currently comes from fossil fuels, a percentage that is unlikely to change soon. Capture and storage of carbon dioxide from power plants and fuel production facilities is necessary for mitigating global warming. Major challenges remain before these technologies can be deployed at scale.

TRANSPORTATION: In transportation, the major challenge is to increase vehicle fuel economy, reduce emissions, and initiate the transition to non-petroleum fuels. We are working on improving combustion engines, developing viable fuel cell and advanced battery systems, and exploring innovative approaches to using hydrogen in engines and to fuel cell-powered vehicles.

BATTERIES AND STORAGE: Energy storage is a significant enabler for expanding the use of renewable energy and for electrification of the transportation system.

BUILDING TECHNOLOGY: In environmental conditioning, the United States per capita energy use is among the highest in the world, in part because the per capita space usage is also high. One important challenge is to apply environmental conditioning only to necessary regions within a space, rather than uniformly throughout the space. Here we are working on small cryogenic systems that can provide precision cooling to small areas. That work is being expanded to scales and temperatures suitable for cooling electronics, sensors, and personal spaces.

Source: From www.web.mit.edu/c21ce/about.html

Check your understanding

1   Give one example of something the Center for 21st Century Energy does.

----

2   Give two of the three areas the next generation will be educated in at the center.

----

3   What is the next frontier in wind energy?

----

4   How much of our energy comes from fossil fuels?

----

5   Why is energy usage per person in the US so high?

6*   Which form of energy in the article interests you most and why?

Language focus

Providing concise responses

When giving short answers, we need to make sure we give enough information to answer the question but not so much that it is unclear whether we have fully understood what is being asked. Read the passage below:

> The Eden Project in Cornwall has created mini biomes in the hope that visitors leave with a better understanding of how they can help their own environment. Nearly one million people visit the Eden Project every year.

What is the best response to the question "How many people visit the Eden Project every year?"

A One million people

B Nearly one million people visit the Eden Project every year

C Nearly one million people

B and C contain all the information necessary but B also gives some unnecessary information. Which bits do you think are not needed?

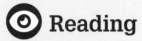 **Reading**

Read the following passage and answer the questions completely and concisely.

When she set up her own company, just before she was 18, Lily knew she wanted to use only ethical ingredients in her face creams. She travelled the world to find farms which were appropriate and which she knew would pay its employees well. She launched her face creams across Europe – ten stores in ten countries – and they soon became a celeb favourite.

1 How old was Lily when she started her company?

----

2 Give one adjective to describe the ingredients Lily used.

----

3 Name two things the farms needed to be.

----

4 How many countries were her creams launched in?

----

5 What sort of person buys the face creams?

 **Recycled clothes**

Going "green" can also be glamorous.

The couture dresses made from recycled materials were created by ethical fashion designer Gary Harvey to launch Recycle Now Week, a government-funded campaign aimed at encouraging more recycling.

The fashion collection includes a "technicolour dream dress", made from recycled cans, bottle tops, cardboard packaging, glass beads, and plastic bags; a "tulle" skirt made from 30 newspapers; and a tiered ball gown made from 42 pairs of used Levi 501s.

New consumer research for Recycle Now Week reveals that over half of us feel guilty for not doing more to protect the environment.

The nation's top causes of "green guilt" are throwing food away (41 per cent), using plastic bags at the supermarket (33 per cent), throwing packaging away instead of recycling (28 per cent), leaving the TV on standby (27 per cent), and travelling short distances in the car instead of walking or cycling (23 per cent).

One supporter said, "These days, I think most of us have a much stronger awareness of how our behaviour impacts on the environment. I've been a keen recycler for several years, and it's great to see that it's no longer a minority activity. In fact, going green has never been more fashionable."

Recycle Now Week sees events across the country, from recycling exhibitions to environmental magicians, composting displays to eco-fashion shows. Local authorities, community groups, supermarkets, and businesses are getting involved.

Source: From www.fashion.telegraph.co.uk/ news-features/TMG3296085/Denise-models- clothes-fashioned-from-recycling.html

Check your understanding

1   Why were the dresses made at first?

----

2   How many pairs of jeans were needed to make the ballgown?

----

3   Which reason comes top for making people feel guilty about how green they are?

----

4   Give one example of something which happens during Recycle Now Week.

----

5   Give two examples of groups involved in Recycle Now Week.

6* Think of one thing you throw away which you could recycle in the future.

Saving energy

🔊 Earth Hour

Earth Hour is a global campaign which encourages people to turn off their lights and other electrical items for one hour, as well as thinking about ways they can reduce the negative impact they may be having on the environment. Watch the video and then answer the following questions.

www.youtube.com/watch?v = 2UywrjnOaUE

Check your understanding

Put one word into each gap to complete what was said.

1 The world is using the equivalent of one and a half _____ to support life on Earth.

2 People are _____ out their lights to signal their concern about the future of our life on this Earth.

3 If _____ people agree to take public transportation instead of their cars for one week, we will climb 96 storeys of this building.

4 The one thing we all _____ is where we live.

5 We can turn the _____ of one hour into the actions of every hour.

💬 Discussion topic

You have committed to Earth Hour and are now about to take part in the "I will if you will" initiative. You have to decide what you are willing to do and how many others have to commit to helping the environment before you will do it. Choose from the list or use your own ideas:

• Pick up all the rubbish in your local area for an hour.

• Do a charity run for an hour.

• Volunteer for a local organization for an hour.